WITHDRAWN

D0231667

Evesham & Malvern Hills College
Library
35672

School Blues

DANIEL PENNAC

School Blues

Translated from the French by
Sarah Ardizzone

With a Foreword by Quentin Blake

MACLEHOSE PRESS
QUERCUS · LONDON

First published in Great Britain in 2010 by
MacLehose Press
an imprint of Quercus
21 Bloomsbury Square
London WC1A 2NS

First published as *Chagrin d'école* by Éditions Gallimard, Paris

This book is supported by the French Ministry of Foreign Affairs,
as part of the Burgess programme run by the Cultural Department
of the French Embassy in London.

It has also been selected to receive financial assistance from the English
PEN's Writers in Translation programme supported by Bloomberg.

A CIP catalogue record for this book is available
from the British Library

ISBN (HB) 978 1 906694 64 7
ISBN (TPB) 978 1 906694 65 4

2 4 6 8 10 9 7 5 3 1

Set in Garamond by Patty Rennie
Printed and bound in Great Britain by Clays Ltd, St Ives plc

For Minne, oh how much!

To Fanchon Delfosse, Pierre Arènes, José Rivaux,
Philippe Bonneu, Ali Mehidi, Françoise Dousset and
Nicole Harlé, rescuers of students nonpareil.
And in memory of Jean Rolin, who never
despaired of the dunce I used to be.

Contents

Foreword

Daniel Pennac has three exemplary qualifications for writing this book. One is that he is an exceptionally good writer, and I know this from having read several of his novels, and even more from the fact that every one of them seems to be a bestseller with his readership in France. Another is that he was for many years a brilliant teacher. I have never seen him in the classroom: I *have* seen him, however, talking to an audience at the Institut Français in London, and performing his own words on stage in Paris and, if you know anything at all about teaching, that wouldn't leave you in much doubt. But in addition to that he wrote a book twenty years ago (another bestseller, needless to say) called *Comme un Roman*, about children and young people and reading, and about his experiences and innovations in the classroom, not least that of reading whole books to his class of reluctant readers – or who thought they were reluctant until he got going. He offers the basic observation, or rule of behaviour, that "a book is not an exam, it is a gift". In that book he also sets out a number of other rules (you don't necessarily have to finish a book, you're allowed to skip, you can identify with the main character . . .), so that when it was newly translated a few years ago (by Sarah Ardizzone, our translator of *School Blues*), it was appropriately called *The Rights of the Reader.*

In *School Blues* Pennac moves from the point of view of the concerned adult to that of the pupil, and it is here that we come to his third and most striking qualification. At school he was a dunce.

In French, the word is *cancre*; what is something of a problem in both French and English is that we are working with an out-of-date vocabulary that doesn't quite apply to modern situations – and more recent colloquialisms (drop-out, klutz, dimmy, no-hoper, make your own list) don't quite do the job either. But, as we see from Daniel Pennac's introductory note, the French *cancre* has greater resonance. His note is just the helpful first step, because the distinctive value of the whole book is that it explores this delinquency and (maybe apparent) dimness from the inside – its frustrations, passions, despair, rebellion and, sometimes, also imaginativeness. It is present for us in this novelist's words as though it's happening and alive for us. There aren't many books about education, I imagine, that affect one's feelings as Pennac's do.

What he brings to the situation of the so-called no-hoper is the prospect of hope. And for that is needed inspiration, discipline, motivation, an understanding of the art of teaching, in other words, good teachers. Perhaps this foreword should end there, but I cannot quite prevent myself adding one more observation from my viewpoint on the edge of education. I may indeed be mistaken, but I have the impression that there is another kind of dunce, one that resists the possibility of rescue. Were these dunces perhaps not even dunces at school but developed the characteristics later? They are in politics and administration; they set targets and introduce initiatives; they write reports in language which is an offence against language; they specialize in failure and exclusion: and all this in an attempt to control an activity which one senses that, fundamentally, they do not understand. I suspect that some of them have even got into the business of education. Or have I just imagined this?

Forgive me if I anticipate and take you forward to p. 14:

> All the bad press school gets simply obscures the number of children it has saved from vice, prejudice, arrogance, ignorance, stupidity and greed, as well as from class-bound or fatalistic families.

We must hope, as we read *School Blues*, that some of the people responsible for the organisation of education will read it too.

Quentin Blake

The *Cancre*, or Dunce

Since 1662 the French word *cancre* has referred to a student who doesn't succeed at school. This comprises an extension of the word's primary meaning: "crab" (1372).

It's a telling metaphor. The dunce is a student who doesn't follow the straight and narrow path of normal schooling; he moves slowly and sideways, far behind the students ahead of him on the path to academic success.

The *cancre* suffers from *cancrerie* (1885), or duncedom. This word – which I also use frequently – has fallen into obsolescence without being replaced. Today, we talk about "no-hopers", about "hopelessness", which makes no sense, pedagogically speaking. For the dunce is not necessarily a "no-hoper". Einstein, Balzac, Chaplin, Edison, Charlemagne, Debussy, Darwin, Picasso and dozens of others were dunces. If they'd been "no-hopers", they'd have stayed that way. Exceptional gifts which school didn't know how to bring out were waiting deep inside their duncedom.

These illustrious exceptions shouldn't disguise the fact that most dunces die – socially – of duncedom. Which takes me back to another illuminating root: the word *cancer* (1478), in the sense of a malignant tumour. Duncedom is a tumour from which certain children suffer, and of which they must be cured, for it can prove fatal to society.

So the dunce is not just a bad student. That he *is* a bad student is, rather, a consequence of being inhibited by his duncedom, as is his potential to be lazy, unruly, violent, a liar, a truant etc. "Bad student" is, then, an inadequate and even an inaccurate translation of *cancre*, since it attempts to pass off consequence for cause.

I

The Dustbin in Djibouti

What can be explained statistically
is complicated personally

I

Let us begin with the epilogue: my mother, nearly a hundred now, watching a film about an author she knows well. We see this author at home in Paris, surrounded by his books, in his library, which is also his study. Its window opens on to a school playground. Recreational rowdiness. We learn that he worked as a teacher for a quarter of a century, and that if he chose this apartment overlooking two school-yards, he did so in the spirit of a railwayman retiring above a marshalling yard. Next we see the author in Spain, in Italy, in conversation with his translators, joking with friends in Venice, walking in the Vercors, a solitary figure at misty altitudes, talking about his craft, about language, style, structure, characterization . . . Another study, this time its window giving on to alpine splendour. These scenes are punctuated by interviews with artists the author admires, and who in turn talk about their own work: the film-maker and novelist Dai Sijie, the cartoonist Sempé, the singer Thomas Fersen, the painter Jürg Kreienbühl.

Back to Paris: the author at his computer, among his dictionaries.

He's passionate about them, he says. We even find out – here the film ends – that he is himself a dictionary entry, in *Robert*, under P for Pennac, full surname Pennacchioni, first name Daniel.

My mother watches this film together with my brother Bernard, who recorded it for her. She watches from start to finish, quite still in her armchair, eyes fixed on the screen, not a squeak out of her, in the failing light.

The film ends.

The credits roll.

Silence.

Then, turning slowly to Bernard, she asks: "D'you think he'll ever come good?"

2

She's never really got over the fact that I was a bad student. Today, as her aged consciousness abandons the beaches of the present and ebbs gently back to the distant archipelagos of memory, the first reefs she encounters remind her of the worry that consumed her throughout my school years.

Resting her concerned gaze on me, slowly: "What is it that you *do*, exactly?"

From early on, my future appeared so compromised that she could never feel entirely confident about my present. Not destined to *become* anything, I wasn't equipped to survive as far as she was concerned. I was her precarious child. And yet, from September 1969, when I entered my first classroom as a teacher, she knew I was able to stand on my own two feet. In the decades that followed, however (meaning my entire adult life), she secretly resisted all "evidence of my success" as attested to by telephone calls, letters, visits, the publication of my books, newspapers articles, even appearances on Pivot. Not the stability of my professional life, not the recognition my writing received, not even things she heard about me from third parties or read in the press could fully reassure her. Yes, she was thrilled by my successes; she discussed them with her friends, agreeing that my father, who had died before knowing about them, would have been pleased, but in the hiding place of her heart dwelt the anxiety spawned by the bad student I'd been. This was how her love for me expressed itself. When I teased her about the delights of maternal concern, she would always retaliate neatly with a Woody Allen joke: "What do you expect? Not all Jewish women are mothers, but all mothers are Jewish!"

Today, no longer fully present, my old Jewish mother betrays that same concern as her eyes come to rest on her sixty-year-old last-born. A concern that may have lost some of its intensity, a fossilized concern reduced to a habit, but one that remains sufficiently resilient for her to ask, her hand on mine, as I'm getting ready to go, "Have you got somewhere to live, in Paris?"

3

So, I was a bad student. Every evening, I would head home with school snapping at my heels. My reports testified to my schoolmasters' disapproval. When I wasn't bottom of the class, I was second to last. (Champagne all round!) At first unreceptive to arithmetic, then to mathematics, suffering from severe spelling difficulties, rebellious when it came to memorizing dates and places, incapable of learning foreign languages, and with a reputation for laziness (lessons not learned, homework not done), I brought home pitiful results unredeemed by music, or sport, or indeed any extra-curricular activity.

"Do you understand? Can't you *understand* what I'm trying to explain to you?"

No, I didn't understand. And this failure to understand stretched so far back into my childhood that my family had dreamt up a creation myth for it: my learning the alphabet. I never stopped hearing about how it had taken me an entire year to learn the letter *A*. The letter *A*, in a year. The desert of my ignorance began to form even before I encountered insurmountable *B*.

"Don't panic, twenty-six years from now he'll be able to recite his alphabet perfectly."

Such was my father's wry humour, intended to distract from his own fears. Many years later, when I was retaking my final year at school in pursuit of the *baccalauréat* that obstinately eluded me, he would offer the following: "Don't worry, even sitting the *bac* becomes second nature in the end."

Or, in September 1968, when at last I had my degree in French Language and Literature under my belt: "You needed a revolution to get your degree; should we expect a world war when you sit your teacher's exams?"

This wasn't meant nastily. It was our way of bonding. From very early on, we chose to put a brave face on things, my father and I.

But let's go back to my beginnings. The last born of four brothers, I was a case apart. My parents hadn't got in any practice with my siblings, whose schooling, if not exceptionally brilliant, had panned out smoothly.

I was an object of amazement, and continual amazement at that, as the years rolled by without any signs of improvement to my educational torpor. "I'm flabbergasted!" and "Well, I'll be damned!" are phrases I associate with adults staring at me in total disbelief, as they registered my failure to get my head round anything at all.

Everyone else understood things more quickly than I did, or so it seemed.

"You're thick as two planks!"

One afternoon during my *bac* year (one of my *bac* years), my father was giving me a trigonometry lesson in the room we used as our library, our dog slyly asleep on the bed behind us. Once spotted, he was curtly dispatched: "Out, dog, off you go to your chair!"

Five minutes later, the dog was back on the bed, having carefully retrieved the old blanket that covered his chair and brought it into the library to lie down on. Applause, of course, and deservedly so: for an animal to make the connection between something forbidden and the abstract notion of cleanliness, reaching the conclusion that he had to make his own bed in order to enjoy the company of his masters – hats off, this was clearly an authentic act of *reasoning*. The lesson I took from this incident was that even our pet dog caught on more quickly than I did. I seem to remember whispering in his ear: "Your turn to go to school tomorrow, arse-licker."

4

Two men of a certain age are walking by the river Loup, the river of their childhood. Two brothers. My brother Bernard and I. Half a century ago, they used to dive into this transparency. They swam among chubs who remained unperturbed by this disturbance of the peace. The familiarity of the fish implying that such happiness would last forever. The river flowed between cliffs. As the brothers followed it to the sea, now carried along by the current, now clambering over rocks, they would sometimes lose sight of each other. To find one another again, they learned to whistle. Endless chirrings echoed off the rock faces.

Today, the water level has dropped, the fish have disappeared, a stagnant slimy froth signals the victory of laundry detergent over nature. All that remains from our childhood is the song of the cicadas and the resinous heat of the sun. Oh, and we can still whistle; we've never been out of hearing range of one another.

I tell Bernard I'm thinking of writing a book about school, not about how school has changed as society has changed, as this river has changed, but about what never changes at the heart of such perpetual disruption, about the kind of permanence I never hear being discussed: *the shared pain of dunces, parents and teachers*, the relationships between those afflicted by school blues.

"That's a huge subject . . . How will you approach it?"

"By grilling you, for example. What do you remember about how rubbish I was at, say . . . maths?"

Bernard was the only family member able to help me with my schoolwork without my clamming up. We shared a bedroom until I was sent away to boarding school at the age of twelve.

"Maths? Well, it all began with arithmetic. One day, I asked you what you were meant to be doing with a fraction you were staring at. 'I've got to find the common denominator,' was your knee-jerk reply. There was only one fraction, so only one denominator, but you stuck to your guns: 'I've got to find the common denominator.' I pressed you further: 'Think about it, Daniel, there's *only one* fraction, so there's *only one* denominator.' You lost your temper: 'But that's what the teacher said: *Always reduce fractions to their common denominator!*'"

And for the rest of their walk, the two men can't stop smiling. That's all in the past now. One has been a teacher for twenty-five years: two thousand five hundred students, give or take, some with "severe learning difficulties", as the expression goes. And both are fathers. So they know all about "That's what the teacher said . . ." Yes, the dunce's trust in the litany. His teacher's words are the floating branches to which the bad student clings in a river whose current is dragging him towards a waterfall. He repeats what the teacher said. Not for it to mean anything or for the rule to make sense, no, just to get out of a tight spot, albeit briefly, to be "left alone". Or to feel loved. At any price.

". . ."

"So, another book about school? You don't think there are enough of them already?"

"Not about school. Everybody is ready to wade in when it comes to school: the eternal quarrel between Ancients and Moderns, about the curriculum, its social role, its aims, about school past and future.

No, I'm planning a book about dunces. About the pain of incomprehension and the damage it can do."

"Was it really so difficult for you?"

". . ."

". . ."

"Tell me more about the dunce I used to be."

"You were always complaining that you couldn't remember anything. The stuff I made you learn vanished into thin air. The next morning, you'd forgotten everything."

That's how it was. In today's youth-speak, I didn't get it. It wouldn't go in and I didn't get it. The simplest words lost their substance as soon as I was asked to learn them. If I had to revise the region of the Jura for homework, for example (more than an example, a memory in fact), then that tiny two-syllable word *Jura* would immediately discombobulate until it no longer had any connection with Franche-Comté, the Ain, clock-making, vineyards, pipes, high altitude, cows, harsh winters, the border with Switzerland or the Alps, or in fact with mountains at all. It ceased to have any meaning. "Jura," I'd repeat to myself, "Jura?" "Jura" – I'd keep saying it over and over again, as indefatigably as a child who won't stop chewing, chewing but not swallowing, repeating but not taking anything in, until taste and meaning are completely reduced to mush, chewing, repeating, Jura, Jura, jura, jura, juw, rah, juw, ra, ju, ra, jurajurajura, until the word becomes an undefined lump without any vestige of meaning, a fuzzy noise inside a drunkard's spongy brain . . . *That's* how you fall asleep over your geography lesson.

"You claimed to be allergic to capital letters."

They were fearsome sentinels, capital letters. Rising up between myself and proper nouns, forbidding me to associate with them. Any word beginning with a capital letter was destined for instant oblivion: towns, rivers, battles, heroes, treaties, poets' names, galaxies, theorems, banished out of mind because of a paralysing capital letter. Halt, the capital letter would call out, do not cross the threshold of this name, it is too *proper* for you, and you are unworthy of it, you cretin!

"Make that a pipsqueak cretin!" Bernard points out as we continue our walk.

Two brothers can be heard laughing.

"Later on, it was exactly the same with foreign languages: I couldn't shake off the idea that what was being said was too clever for me."

"Which got you out of having to learn vocabulary lists."

"English words were as volatile as proper nouns . . ."

". . ."

". . ."

"So basically, you lied to yourself."

"Yes, that's the prerogative of dunces, to keep on telling themselves the lie of their duncedom: I'm a no-hoper, I'll never make it, there's no point even trying, I don't stand a chance, I've already told you, it wasn't meant to be, school and me . . . To dunces, school resembles a members-only club from which they bar themselves. Aided and abetted by the occasional teacher.

". . ."

". . ."

Two men of a certain age walking by a river. At the end of their walk they come to a lake surrounded by reeds and pebbles.

"Still a dab hand at ducks and drakes?" asks Bernard.

5

There is, of course, the question of root cause. How did I become a dunce in the first place? Child of a middle-class civil servant, born into a close, loving family, surrounded by responsible adults who helped with my homework . . . My father was a *polytechnicien*, my mother a housewife, no divorce, no alcoholism, no emotionally disturbed relatives, no hereditary defects, three brothers who had all passed the *baccalauréat* (all mathematicians; two became engineers, the third an army officer), normal family routine, healthy diet, books in the home, cultural interests commensurate with background and era (father and mother both born before 1914): painting up to the Impressionists, poetry up to Mallarmé, music up to Debussy, Russian novels, a predictable phase of reading Teilhard de Chardin, Joyce and Cioran if they were feeling really adventurous, calm, laughter-filled and cultivated mealtime discussions.

Despite all this, a dunce.

It's not as if an explanation can be found in our family history either: a fine example of progress across three generations thanks to a secular, free and compulsory education system, a true republican rise through the ranks, in short, a victory for Jules Ferry . . . Another Jules, my father's uncle Jules Pennacchioni, "The Uncle", guided the children of Guargualé and Pila-Canale, the Corsican villages from which our family came, through to school certificates; we have The Uncle to thank for generations of primary-school teachers, postmen, police officers and other civil servants across colonial and metropolitan France . . . (perhaps a few bandits too, but at least he'd have made them into readers). The Uncle imposed dictation and calculus on everyone regardless of circumstances, or so they say; they also say that he went so far as to round up children whose parents kept them away from school during the chestnut harvest. He'd retrieve those kids from the Corsican *maquis*, take them home with him and warn their slave-driver fathers: "You'll get your son back when he's got his certificate!"

If it's a myth, it's one I like. I don't see how being a teacher can be thought of in any other way. All the bad press school gets simply obscures the number of children it has saved from vice, prejudice, arrogance, ignorance, stupidity and greed, as well as from class-bound or fatalistic families.

So that was The Uncle.

And yet, three generations later, me: The Dunce.

He'd have been The Uncle Undone, if he'd known . . . Luckily, he died before I was born.

Not only did my ancestors rule out my being a dunce, but, as the last representative of an increasingly qualified line, I was intended to become the family's crown jewel: *polytechnicien* or *normalien, énarque* of course, *la Cour des comptes,* who could say . . . One hoped for nothing less. Alongside this career, an efficient marriage resulting in children destined to cram at Louis-le-Grand, then to be propelled towards the Elysée Palace or at least the executive directorship of some global cosmetics consortium. The cycle of social Darwinism, the reproduction of elites . . .

Well, no, actually: a dunce.

A dunce without historical precedent, sociological justification or disillusionment: a dunce in his own right. A bog standard dunce.

Why?

Perhaps an educational psychologist would have the answer, but this was before the era when such specialists became family surrogates. We made do with what we had to hand.

Bernard ventured this explanation: "When you were six, you fell into a municipal dustbin in Djibouti."

"When I was six? The year I learned the letter *A*?"

"Yes. You fell off a wall into an open-air rubbish tip. I don't remember how long you spent marinating down there. You disappeared, we looked for you everywhere, and all the while you were boiling in close to 140-degree heat. I'd rather not think about it."

The image of the dustbin is apt enough for a student lost to the school system like so much flotsam and jetsam. In fact *dustbin* is a word I've heard muttered numerous times in reference to those private, unregulated establishments that take in the dregs from other secondary schools. I boarded at one from the age of twelve to seventeen. (Among the teachers I endured there, four conspired to rescue me.)

"By the time we'd got you out of that rubbish dump, you'd developed septicaemia; months of penicillin jabs followed. You were sick as a dog and scared witless. Every time the male nurse showed up, we'd spend hours looking for you. One day, you hid in a wardrobe that fell on top of you."

Fear of being injected, now there's a telling metaphor: my entire school career was spent running away from teachers whom I thought of as quacks out of Molière, armed with outsized syringes and tasked with inoculating me with the penicillin of the '50s, which I remember *very* well – a sort of molten lead.

In any event, yes, fear was the single most important factor of my schooling, its padlock. For the teacher I became, allaying the fears of my worst students was a matter of urgency, to force that lock open so that learning might stand a chance of squeezing through.

6

I'm dreaming. Not a dream from childhood, a dream in the present, while I'm writing this book. Truth is, I had it just after I wrote the last chapter. I'm sitting in my pyjamas on the edge of my bed. Enormous plastic numbers, like the ones small children play with, are scattered across the carpet. I have to "put these numbers in order". Those are my instructions. I'm happy; it seems an easy task. I lean over and reach for the numbers. That's when I notice that my hands have disappeared. There aren't any hands where my pyjamas end. My sleeves are empty. I panic, not because my hands have disappeared, but because I can't reach the numbers to put them in order. Which I would have known how to do.

7

And yet, to all appearances I was a lively and playful child, without being manic. A mean hand at marbles and jacks, unbeatable at dodge ball, world champion at pillow fights, I was always playing. A chatterbox who liked to laugh, a clown even, I made friends at every level of classroom society, with dunces of course, but with brain-boxes too – I wasn't prejudiced. More than anything, it was my cheerfulness that certain teachers held against me. Not content with being hopeless, I was insolent to boot. The least a dunce could do was to be discreet about it: stillborn being the ideal. But liveliness was my life-blood, so to speak. Being playful rescued me from the blues whenever I slumped back into loneliness and shame.

My God, the loneliness of the dunce, ashamed of never being able to *do what you're supposed to be doing.* And that urge to run away . . . I felt the urge to run away very early on. But where to? Not sure. To run away from myself, if you like, but also *into* myself. A version of me that was acceptable to others. I owe the strange writing that preceded my handwriting to this urge to run away. Instead of forming letters, I would draw little stick-men who went running into the margin, where they'd form a gang. Not that I didn't apply myself at the beginning. I had a reasonable stab at joining up my letters, but, little by little, they transformed themselves into tiny, joyful, leaping beings who went off to frolic elsewhere, ideograms representing my need to feel alive:

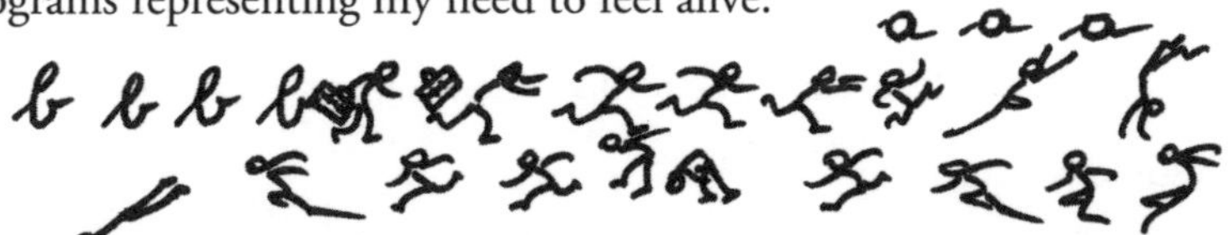

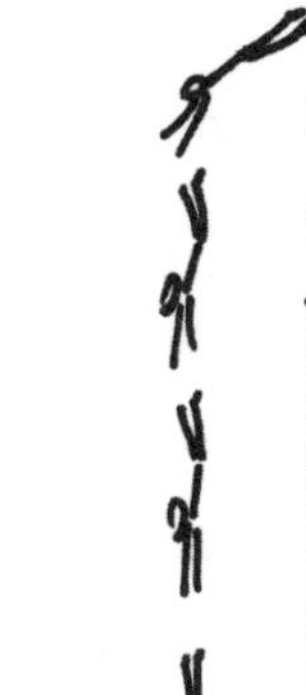

I still use these little stick-men today. They're invaluable for rescuing me from the requisite platitudes when I'm signing review copies for journalists. They're my childhood gang, and I remain loyal to them.

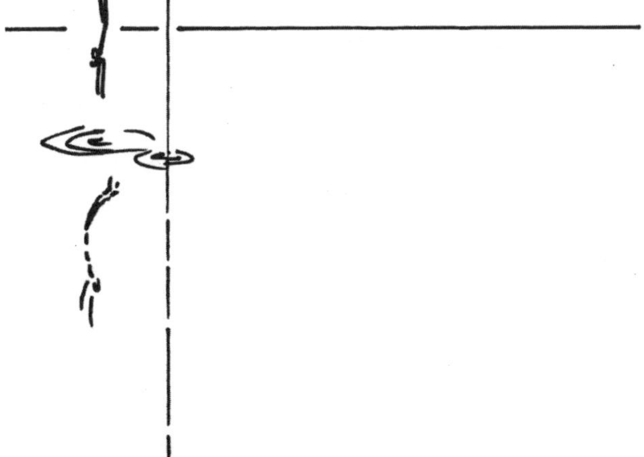

8

As a teenager, I dreamed of a gang more real. I was in the wrong era, from the wrong background, and my situation ruled it out, but to this day I maintain I'd have joined a gang, given half a chance. In fact, I'd have *leapt* at it. My playmates weren't up to the challenge. As far as they were concerned, I only existed at break-time; in class, I was made to feel like an alien. My dream was to become part of a gang where school counted for nothing.

What's the attraction of gangs? Losing yourself in the belief that you're finding yourself. The illusion of identity. Anything to forget your alienation from school, to escape the contemptuous gaze of adults. How those looks all blur into one! To pit a sense of community against perpetual loneliness, somewhere else against here, turf against solitude. To leave Dunce Island, even if that means on board a pirate ship ruled by the law of the fist and you end up, at best, in prison. The others – teachers, adults – all seemed so much stronger than I was, and their strength, more devastating than the fist, was so acknowledged, so sanctioned, that my hunger for revenge bordered on the obsessive. (Four decades later, I wasn't surprised when I heard the phrase "*avoir la haine*" issuing from the mouths of certain teenagers. It expressed the need for revenge I'd felt myself only too keenly, albeit multiplied by many new sociological, cultural and economic factors.)

Fortunately, my playmates weren't the sort to join gangs, and I didn't grow up in the inner city. So I was a gang unto myself, as Renaud's song has it, a modest gang, carrying out my own underhand reprisals. Those ox tongues, for example (a hundred of them), removed from their tins in the canteen under cover of darkness and nailed to the bursar's door because he served them up twice a week and we'd find them on our plates the following lunchtime if we hadn't eaten them the day before. Or the kipper tied to the exhaust pipe of an English teacher's brand-new car (an Ariane saloon, I remember, the walls of the tyres as white as a pimp's shoes . . .), which then stank so badly of grilled fish that the classroom began to reek as soon as he walked through the door. Or those thirty hens filched from the farms close to my boarding school in the mountains, in order to populate the housemaster's bedroom the weekend he grounded me. That room was turned into a most glorious henhouse: droppings and feathers stuck together, straw to make it authentic, broken eggs everywhere and a generous scattering of corn on top. And the smell! It was some party when the unsuspecting housemaster opened the door, releasing those crazed female prisoners into the corridors with all the house residents chasing in their wake.

This was idiotic behaviour, of course, idiotic, malicious, reprehensible, unforgivable . . . And inefficient, with it: the kind of abuse that does nothing to improve the character of the teaching staff . . . That said, to my dying day I'll never regret my hens, my kipper or my poor oxen with their severed tongues. Along with my crazy little stick-men, they all belonged to my gang.

9

Here is a pedagogical constant: with a few rare exceptions, the lonely avenging student (or the sly, rowdy one, depending on your point of view) never owns up. And if someone else did it, not him, he doesn't squeal either. Is this solidarity? Not necessarily. It's more a visceral pleasure at seeing authority exhaust itself in sterile lines of enquiry. The fact that an entire classroom will be punished – deprived of this or that – until the guilty party gives himself up doesn't affect the avenging student. Quite the opposite, as it happens, since he gets to feel part of the community at last. He joins in with the general consensus that it's "disgusting" to make so many "innocent students" "pay" for the behaviour of a single "guilty party". His sincerity is astounding. The fact that he himself is the guilty party is irrelevant. By punishing everybody, the authorities have allowed him to switch sides; this is no longer about facts but about principles. And, being a good teenager, fairness is a principle on which he refuses to budge.

"They don't know who did it, so they're making us all pay; it stinks."

To be called a coward, a thief, a liar, or anything else for that matter, to have a booming "prosecutor" publicly declare his contempt for the flaming idiot who "doesn't even have the courage to own up to what he's done" – none of this affects the avenging student. Firstly, because what's being said to him merely confirms what has been said to him a thousand times already, and anyway he agrees with the "prosecutor" (it's an unfamiliar pleasure, this secret acquiescence: *Yes, you're right, I'm as evil as you say I am, worse in fact, if you only knew . . .*). Secondly, because the "prosecutor" wouldn't have had the courage to hang the housemaster's gowns from the lightning rod, nor was any student present bold enough to do so; no, he did it, he alone, in the dead of night, in his nocturnal solitude made glorious. For a few hours, those gowns became a black pirate's flag flying above the school, and no-one would ever know who had hoisted that grotesque standard aloft.

And if somebody else gets blamed instead of him, well, all the more reason to keep quiet, because he understands how the world works, and knows (like Claudel, whom he'll never read, by the way) that "one can also deserve injustice".

He doesn't confess. Because there's a sense to his loneliness now; at last he can stop feeling frightened. He no longer keeps his eyes lowered. Behold the guilty party with the honest stare. This one-off pleasure buried in his silence: *nobody will ever find out.* When you don't think you belong anywhere, you become your own audience.

What he relishes, more than anything else, is the dark joy of becoming unfathomable to those who are academically well-equipped and who criticize him for not knowing his arse from his elbow. In short, he's discovered a talent for frightening people who frighten him. It gives him a real buzz. Nobody knows what he's *capable* of, and that's how he likes it.

Delinquency is born when all of one's intelligence is invested in cunning.

10

But limiting ourselves to my clandestine acts of revenge gives a false impression of the kind of student I was. (In any case, the headmaster's gowns weren't my doing.) Much as I might like to depict myself as a perfect caricature (the gleeful dunce, nightly hatching feats of revenge . . . the invisible Zorro of childish punishments . . .), I was also – and most importantly – a kid ready to compromise anything and everything to win a benevolent look from an adult. Furtive in my solicitation of teachers' approval, I nonetheless went by the book: *Yes, sir, you're right, sir . . . No, sir, I'm not as stupid as all that, sir, no, not as bad, not as disappointing, not as . . .* How humiliating, when a teacher's cutting remark plunged me back into worthlessness. How uplifting, when he proffered two kind words, which I immediately stashed away as a gem of humanity . . . How I rushed home that same evening to tell my parents: "I had a nice chat with Mr So-and-So . . ." (As if, my father must have thought to himself, and with good reason, what really mattered was having a "nice chat" . . .)

I dragged this tail of shame behind me for a very long time.

Beginning with my first failures, I was hostage to both a sense of hatred and the need for affection. It was a case of mollifying the ogre that was School. I'd do anything to stop him gobbling up my heart. Which explains why, aged eleven, I had to contribute towards my teacher's birthday present, even though he only ever gave me negative marks on my dictations: "Minus 38, Pennacchioni, the temperature keeps on dropping!" I racked my brains for something the bastard would genuinely appreciate, organized the whip-round and made good the shortfall on our terrible purchase.

In those days, safes were a feature of most bourgeois households. I undertook to pick the lock on my parents' safe in order to contribute to my torturer's present. It was one of those small, dark, squat safes with family secrets asleep inside. A key, a numerical combination lock, then an alphabetical one. I knew where my parents kept the key, but it took me several nights to crack the combination. Combination, key, closed door. Combination, key, closed door. Closed door. Closed door. You think you'll never get there. Then, all of a sudden, click, the door opens. You're stunned. A door has opened on to the secret world of adults. Sensible secrets, in this instance: a few bonds, I imagine, snoozing Russian loans awaiting resurrection, a great uncle's service handgun, its cartridge fully loaded but the firing pin filed down, and money too, not much, a few notes, from which I took the cut necessary to help finance the teacher's present.

Stealing to buy the affection of adults . . . Not exactly theft, and of course it didn't buy me affection. My dark secret was discovered when, that same year, I gave my mother one of those ghastly bonsai trees that were fashionable at the time and which cost an arm and a leg.

There were three upshots to my theft. My mother wept (a rare event), convinced she'd brought a safe-breaker into the world (and this the only domain in which her last-born was unequivocally precocious); I was sent away to boarding school; and for the rest of my life I was incapable of stealing, even in an era when youngsters believed that theft was socially acceptable.

II

To all those who attribute today's youth gangs to the phenomenon of the *banlieues*, I say: Yes, you're right, unemployment, yes, marginalized communities, yes, ethnic ghettoization, yes, the tyranny of designer brands, yes, one-parent families, yes, the growth of a parallel economy and trafficking of every kind, yes, yes, yes . . . But let's not underestimate the one thing we can do something about, which goes back to the dawn of pedagogical time: the loneliness, the shame, of the student who doesn't understand, lost in a world where everyone else does.

We can help him and her out of that prison, whether we're trained to do so or not.

The teachers who rescued me – and who made a teacher out of me – weren't trained to do so. They didn't bother with the origins of my academic frailty. They didn't waste time looking for the causes, much less lecturing me. They were grown-ups confronted with teenagers at risk. They recognized this as a matter of urgency. They took the plunge. They failed. They dived in again, day after day, again and again . . . They pulled me out in the end. And plenty of others too. They literally fished us out. We owe them our lives.

12

As I rummage through the jumble of my old papers in search of my school reports and certificates, I come upon a letter kept by my mother. It is dated February 1959.

I had turned fourteen three months earlier. And I was writing to her from my first boarding school:

Dearest Mother,

I saw my marks too, it's sickening, I've had it up to hear [*sic*], when you work a 2 hr study period non-stop to get 1/20 for your algebra homework witch [*sic*] you thought you'd got right, it's enough to put you of [*sic*], plus I dropt [*sic*] everything to revise for my exams and my 4/20 in functions is because I revised for my geology exam during my maths leson [*sic*] . . .

I'm not clever or hard-working enough to go on with my studies. I'm just not interested, I get hedaches [*sic*] from being stuk [*sic*] inside with all this paperwork, I dont [*sic*] understand anything in English, or algebra, I'm hopeliss [*sic*] at spelling, what's left?

Marie-Thé, the hairdresser in our village, La Colle-sur-Loup, and a friend I've looked up to ever since I was a baby, recently confessed that my mother had poured out her feelings from beneath the plastic hood of the salon hairdryer, confiding her concern about my future. Getting my brothers to promise that they'd take care of me, once she and my father were gone, had brought her a little relief, however.

In the same letter, I wrote: "You've had three clever hard-working boys . . . and another who's a dunce, a laisybones [*sic*] . . ." This was followed by a comparison of my brothers' performances with my own, and strenuous demands for the bloodshed to stop, for me to be taken out of school and sent "to the colonies" (a military family, ours) "in some godfawsaken [*sic*] spot and that wood [*sic*] be the only place where Id [*sic*] be happy". Exiled to the world's end, the stopgap of my dreams, a Bardamu-style escape plan hatched in the mind of a soldier's son.

Ten years later, on 30 September 1969, I received a letter from my father, addressed to the secondary school where I'd been working for a month as a teacher. It was my first job and his first letter to the son who had *become* something. Just out of hospital, he related the small pleasures of his convalescence, including his slow walks with our dog; he gave me the family news, telling me of my cousin's prospective marriage in Stockholm; and he made discreet allusions to the novel which we'd discussed (and which I still haven't written). He was clearly curious to find out what I talked about with my colleagues; he cursed the postal strike, since he was waiting for Angelo Rinaldi's *La Loge du gouverneur* to be sent to him, but sang the praises of Salinger's *Catcher in the Rye* as well as *Le Jardin des délices* by José Cabanis; he apologized for my mother not writing (". . . she's more tired than I am from looking after me"), announced that he had lent the spare tyre of our 2C.V. to my friend Fanchon ("Bernard was delighted to change it for her") and signed off by reassuring me about his health.

He didn't make the slightest reference to my past as a dunce, just as he'd never once threatened me with a calamitous future during my career at school. His tone was as modestly wry as ever, and he didn't appear to find anything astonishing in my new status as a teacher, or think that I should be congratulated, or that anyone should be concerned for my students.

My father was just being himself, a wise ironist, keen to swap banter with me, at a respectable distance, about life's little details.

I have in front of me the envelope in which that letter arrived.

Today, for the first time, I'm struck by a particular detail.

He wasn't content to write my name on the envelope, along with the name of the school, and the street and the town . . .

He added a qualifier: *teacher*.

Daniel Pennacchioni

Teacher at . . .

Teacher . . .

In his meticulous handwriting.

It has taken me a lifetime to hear that shout of joy – and that sigh of relief.

II

Becoming

I'm twelve and a half,

and I haven't done anything with my life

I

As I write these lines, the season of emergency telephone calls is upon us. From March onwards, the phone rings at home more often than usual: distraught friends trying to find a new school for a child who's failing, desperate cousins in search of the umpteenth educational establishment after the umpteenth expulsion, neighbours saying they can't see the point of keeping a student back a year, people I don't know but who claim to know me, they got my phone number from So-and-So . . .

They tend to ring in the evening, towards the end of supper, in the hour of their distress. More often than not it's the mother who calls. It's rarely the father; the father comes into it later, if at all, but to begin with, that first telephone call, it's always the mother, and nearly always on behalf of her son. Apparently, her daughter is more sensible.

Imagine you're the mum. Home alone, supper over, washing up still to be done, your son's school report in front of you, this boy who's sitting in front of a video game having double-locked his bedroom door, unless he's just headed off, despite being tentatively grounded, hanging out with his mates . . . Alone, your hand on the phone, you hesitate. Having to explain your son's situation for the umpteenth time, outlining the history of his failures yet again, you're so tired of it, dear God . . . Experience has taught you what an exhausting path lies ahead: canvassing schools that might offer him a place . . . taking a day off work, from the office, the shop . . . meetings with various heads . . . a barrage of secretaries . . . forms to fill out . . . waiting for replies . . . interviews . . . with the son, without the son . . . tests . . . waiting for results . . . producing all the right documentation . . . dithering – is this school better than that school? (For when it comes to schools, the question of excellence gets asked at the bottom of the abyss as well as at the top of the ladder, not just the best school for the best students but also the best school for those who are failing.) Finally, you make the call. You apologize for disturbing him, you know how often he must get asked these questions, but you've got this son, see, I mean, we just don't know what to do with him any more . . .

Dear teachers, please spare a thought for your colleagues when, in the silence of the staffroom, you write on reports that "the third term will be make or break". Because my phone starts ringing immediately:

"The third term, come off it! They've already made their minds up."

"The third term, the third term, the kid's simply not bothered by this threat of a third term; none of his terms have ever been satisfactory."

"The third term . . . How do they expect him to catch up by then, when he's already this far behind? They know their third term is like a piece of Swiss cheese, with all those holidays in it!"

"If they keep him back again, I'm going to appeal!"

"By then it'll be too late to start looking for a new school . . ."

And so it goes until the end of June, when the third term is indeed make or break – the kid isn't allowed to move up with his class – and, sure enough, it's too late to look for a new school because everybody got there ahead of you, but what can you do, you clung to your hopes, you thought that perhaps this time your son would get the point, he'd really knuckled down this term, yes, yes, no, honestly, he was making an effort, better attendance record . . .

2

There's the dispirited mother, worn out by her child going off the rails, who blames the apparent fallout of conjugal tragedy: when we separated, he . . . ever since his father died, he hasn't been quite . . . There's the mother humiliated by the advice of friends whose children are doing very well, thank you, or worse, who avoid the subject altogether with a discretion verging on insult . . . There's the aggrieved mother, convinced that her son has always been the innocent victim of a coalition of teachers, irrespective of subject; it started early on, at nursery school, a female teacher who . . . and things didn't pick up in the first year of primary school; his teacher, a man this time, was worse, and, would you believe it, by the time he was fourteen, his French teacher went and . . . There's the one who thinks this isn't about particular individuals, who rants about society falling apart, about foundering schools, about a system that's rotten at the core – in short, about the real world not measuring up to her expectations . . . There's the mother who's furious with her child: this boy who has everything but does nothing, who does nothing but expects everything, this boy we've done everything for and who never . . . no, not once, can you believe it! There's the mother who hasn't spoken to a single teacher all year long, and the one who has besieged all of them . . . There's the mother who telephones you to take her son off her hands just like she did last year, the same son she won't want to hear about again until next year, same date, same time, same telephone call, and who says as much: "We'll see where we are next year, but for now we've just got to find him a new school." There's the mother who fears the father's reaction: "This time my husband won't stand for it" (most of the son's school reports having been hidden from the husband in question) . . . There's the mother who doesn't understand why this son is so different from his brother; she makes a concerted effort not to love him any less, does her best to be the same mum for her two boys. Then there's the mother who can't help giving this one special treatment ("I put *everything* into our relationship"), much to his brothers' and sisters' annoyance, of course, and who has exhausted all the resources on offer without success: sport, child psychology, speech therapy, relaxation therapy, vitamin supplements, calming exercises, homeopathy, family and individual counselling . . . There's the mother steeped in psychology who has an explanation for everything and, to her amazement, a solution for nothing; she's the only person in the world who understands her son, her daughter, her son's or daughter's friends, and, with her perpetually youthful outlook ("Age is all in the mind, isn't it?"), she is stunned to discover that the world should have become such an old fogey, so incapable of understanding young people. There's the mother in tears, who calls you and cries silently, and apologizes for crying . . . a mixture of feeling blue, of worry and shame . . . The truth of the matter is they're all a bit ashamed, and they're all worried about their sons' futures: "But what will *become of him*?" Most of them project the present on to the haunting screen of the future in order to construct a version of what lies ahead. This is the great fear of mothers: the future looming like a screen on to which images of a hopeless present, disproportionately enlarged, are projected.

3

What they don't realize is that they're talking to the youngest safe-breaker of his generation, and that if their version of what lies ahead had any basis in fact, I wouldn't be on the telephone listening to them but counting my fleas in prison. This is the film my poor mother must have projected on to the screen of my future when she discovered that her eleven-year-old son was looting the family savings.

So, I offer up a funny story:

"Do you know the only way to make God laugh?"

A pause at the other end of the line.

"Tell him your plans."

In other words, don't panic; nothing ever turns out as expected. This is the only thing the future teaches us, as it becomes the past.

It's not enough, of course, it's like sticking a plaster on a gaping wound, but I'm doing what I can, given the limits of telephonic communication.

4

To be fair, they do sometimes want to talk to me about good students too. The methodical mother, for example, on the lookout for the best school for her child to gain entry to a *grande école* – just as, the moment he was born, she was busy looking for the best nursery – and who kindly imagines that I'm especially well qualified to catch fish at altitude. Or the mother who comes from another country, a first-generation migrant, the caretaker of my apartment block, who's become aware of her daughter's unusual gifts, and she's right, the girl really must pursue higher education, no doubt about it, she's top-notch, clearly going to excel in whatever subject she decides to study . . . (As it turns out, she's currently finishing her law degree.) Then, there's L. M., a farmer in the Vercors, summoned by the village primary-school teacher to discuss his son's brilliant results . . .

"So she asks me what I'd like to see him doing later on."

He raises his glass to toast my good health: "You're a funny lot, you teachers, with all your questions . . ."

"So what did you say to her?"

"What's a father meant to say? The top job, of course. President of France!"

Then there's the other extreme, another father, a cleaning operative who's desperate to curtail his son's studies and send him out to work so he can start earning straight away. ("Another wage in the family would come in handy!") Yes, but here's the thing: the kid wants to be a primary-school teacher, and I think it's a great idea, I'd love him to go into teaching, this boy's so quick and has a real appetite for it, negotiations, negotiations, the happiness of the future students of this future colleague is at stake . . .

Oh dear, now I'm pinning my hopes on the future, yes, me too, reasserting my faith in the egalitarian values of the French educational system. After all, it's the same system that afforded my father an education, and, eighty years on, this boy reminds me of how my father must have been, the little Corsican from Aurillac, around 1913, when his older brother went out to work in order to give the younger brother the means and the time to cross the threshold of the *école polytechnique.*

Then again, I've always encouraged my liveliest friends and students to become teachers. I've always thought that teachers are what make a school. After all, who rescued me from school, if not a handful of teachers?

5

An irritated father tells me, in no uncertain terms: "My son is immature."

He is young and sits stiffly, respecting the angles of his suit. Upright in his chair, he insists that his son is immature. It's a statement inviting neither query nor commentary. It demands a solution, full stop. All the same, I ask how old the boy is.

Instant response: "Already eleven."

I'm not on great form. Perhaps I slept badly. Resting my head in my hands, I declare, like some infallible Rasputin: "I have the answer."

He cocks an eyebrow. Looks satisfied. Good, we're talking professional to professional. Well, out with it then, this solution.

"You must wait," I proclaim.

He's not happy. The conversation isn't going anywhere.

"The kid simply can't go on spending all his time playing!"

The next day, I run into the same father in the street. Same suit, same stiffness, same briefcase.

But he's riding a child's scooter.

That really happened, I swear it did.

6

No future.

Children who won't *become* anything.

Hopeless cases.

When I was at primary school, then *collège* and finally *lycée,* I too possessed an unshakeable belief that I had no future.

It's the very first thing of which a bad student convinces himself.

"What do you expect, with marks like that?"

"You don't seriously think you'll be allowed to move up a class with everyone else, at the end of this school year?" (And all the subsequent years of secondary schooling . . .)

"How do you rate your chances of passing the *bac*? Come on, do me a favour, work it out, what are your chances, out of a hundred?"

Or that headmistress of my *collège* who shrieked with joy: "You, Pennacchioni, pass your B.E.P.C.? You'll never do it! Do you hear me? Never!"

She was quivering with rage.

At least I won't turn out a mad old bag like you! I'll never be a teacher: you're just spiders caught in your own webs, prison guards chained to your desks until the end of time. Never! We students move on, but you're stuck. We're free to leave, but you're banged up for life. We may be bad students going nowhere, but at least we're going! The shape of our lives isn't defined by a teacher's desk!

Matching contempt with contempt, I used to cling to this small comfort: we leave, the teachers stay on; it's a frequent topic of discussion among those sitting at the back of the class. Dunces gorge on words.

What I didn't realize was that there are some teachers who also feel condemned for life: repeating the same lessons forever, in front of classes that blur into one, collapsing under the daily burden of exercise books (can't you just picture Sisyphus pushing a load of exercise books up his hill?). I wasn't aware that monotony is the primary reason cited by teachers who decide to leave the profession. I never imagined that some of them really do suffer from staying put while their students move on . . . I didn't know that teachers worry about the future too: it's time to knuckle down and pass my *agrégation*, to complete my thesis, to get a university teaching job, to fly off to the academic summits of prep classes for the *grandes écoles*, to opt for research, to relocate abroad, to do something creative, to switch to the private sector, to ditch these spotty, dull, vindictive kids and the reams of paper they produce. I didn't know that when teachers aren't thinking about their own futures, they're thinking of their children's futures, of their offspring's higher education . . . I didn't realize that teachers' heads are full to bursting with the future. I just thought they were there to block mine.

A blocked future.

Having replayed it to myself so often, I had rather a specific vision of my life with no future. It wasn't that time would stop, or that the future didn't exist, no, it was that I would be the same as I already was. Not exactly the same, of course, it wouldn't be as if time had stood still, but as if the years had stacked up without anything changing inside me, as if my future moment risked being identical to my present one. So what constituted my present? A feeling of unworthiness that swamped the sum of moments past. I was a nothing, and that's all I had ever been. Yes, time would pass, yes, I'd grow up, yes, things would happen, yes, life would go on, but I'd get through my time on earth without ever achieving any results. This was much more than a certainty, it was me.

Some children are quick to persuade themselves of this notion in the absence of anyone to disabuse them, and since we can't live without passion, they develop, for lack of anything better, a passion for failure.

7

The future, that peculiar threat . . .

A winter's evening. Nathalie rushes down the stairs in floods of tears. School blues that insist on being heard, echoing in the concrete stairwell. She's still a child, the weight of her small body bouncing off each noisy step. It's half past five and nearly all the students have gone home. I'm one of the last teachers to be passing that way. Drumming of feet on stairs, a fresh outburst of sobbing: Oh dear, thinks the teacher in me, school blues – unwieldy blues, blues blown out of proportion. Nathalie appears at the bottom of the stairs. Hey, hey, Nathalie, hey, come on, what's the matter? I know her. She was in my class last year. An unconfident eleven-year-old who often needed reassuring. What's wrong, Nathalie? She doesn't want to say: Nothing, sir, nothing. Well, Nathalie, that's a lot of noise to be making about nothing, isn't it? More floods of tears and then, finally, between gasps, Nathalie lays bare her unhappiness: "Si . . . Si . . . Sir . . . I juss . . . I just . . . I just don't . . . don't under . . . I just *don't understand* . . ."

"Understand what? What is it you don't understand?"

"Thesub . . . thesub . . ."

All of a sudden the cork flies out:

"Subordinate clauses!"

Silence.

Don't laugh.

Whatever you do, don't laugh.

"Subordinate clauses? You're getting all worked up because of subordinate clauses?"

"The subordinate clause of con . . . con . . . concession and opposition."

Relief. The teacher in me thinks quickly and seriously about the type of clause in question. How can I explain to her that there's no need to make a mountain out of this particular molehill? That she uses this lousy clause (one of my favourites, as it happens, if you can have a favourite type of subordinate clause) without thinking about what she's doing. It's the cornerstone of rational argument, a prerequisite for the subtle expression of any point of view, genuine or otherwise. Of course, there can be no tolerance without listening to other points of view. Nathalie, your job is to list the conjunctions that introduce this type of subordinate clause: *though, although, even though, whereas.* By using words like these, you'll learn how to express the niceties of ideas: you'll be running with the hare *and* chasing with the hounds. This type of clause will make a considered, thoughtful young woman of you, prepared to listen and weigh your replies, a woman who can justify her point of view, a philosopher even – that's what the subordinate clause of concession and opposition will do for you!

The teacher's getting into his stride now: how can I console this kid with a grammar lesson? Let's see . . . Have you got five minutes, Nathalie? Then follow me and I'll explain. Here, this classroom is free, sit down, listen carefully, it's easy . . . She sits, she listens, and it really is very easy. Alright? Did you follow that? Now it's your turn. She gives me an example. It's spot on. She's understood. Good. Feeling better? Well, no, actually, not at all, Nathalie bursts into tears again, wracking great sobs, and suddenly she blurts out these words, which I've never forgotten: "You don't understand, sir, I'm twelve and a half, and I haven't done anything with my life!"

". . ."

Later, at home, that sentence keeps going round in my head. What did the kid mean by it? "I haven't done anything . . ." You've done nothing *wrong*, innocent Nathalie, that's for sure.

I have to wait until the following evening to learn that Nathalie's father has just been made redundant after ten years of good and loyal service as a middle manager in some company or other. He's one of the first managers to be made redundant. These are the mid-1980s; until now, unemployment has been the preserve of unskilled workers, if I can put it like that. But this young man, who never doubted his role as a model manager and an attentive father (I'd seen him several times the previous year, concerned about his daughter, who was so shy, so lacking in self-confidence), has gone to pieces. He's done a final reckoning. At family mealtimes he keeps on saying: "I'm thirty-five years old, and I haven't done anything with my life."

8

Nathalie's father ushered in an era when the future itself appeared to have no future. A decade during which students were told, every day and in every way: Hey kids, forget about the good times, they're *over.* No more casual sex, either. Unemployment and A.I.D.S. all round, that's your future. Yes, that's what we parents and teachers drummed into them in order to "motivate" them. A message cheery as a cloudy sky. And that's why young Nathalie was so upset. She could sense the despair in store for her, she was weeping for her future as the youthful dead. And she thought her problems with grammar were to blame for making things even worse. True, she wasn't helped by a teacher who had told her that her head was "filled with dishwater". Dishwater, Nathalie? Let's have a listen . . . Playing the conscientious quack, I jiggle her little head. No, no, there's no water in there, and no dishes either. She manages a shy smile. *Hold on a minute* . . . I rap on her skull with the crook of my index finger, as if knocking on a door. No, that's a very fine brain you've got in there, Nathalie, exceptional even. It makes a beautiful sound, the sound of a head filled with ideas! Finally, she giggles.

What sadness we imposed on their souls during those years. And how I prefer the laughter of Marcel Aymé, Marcel's good old rotten laugh, when he boasts about his son's shrewdness at sniffing out unemployment before anyone else:

> "Émile, you've been a lot smarter than your brother. But then you're older and you understand how life is. At any rate, I'm not worried about you; you've resisted temptation, and since you've never lifted a finger, you're all set for what lies ahead. You see, the hardest thing if you're unemployed is not being brought up for it. The itch to work is in all of us; it's stronger than we are. But I can rest easy about you: you're bone idle, always will be."
>
> "Come off it," complained Émile, "I can read – well, nearly."
>
> "That just goes to show how smart you are. You haven't made any effort, or picked up that nasty habit of working, but you'll still be able to follow the Tour de France in your newspaper, along with the great sporting events that get written up as fodder for the unemployed. Oh yes, you'll be a happy man . . ."

9

More than twenty years have passed. Today, unemployment affects all levels of society, a secure professional future no longer beckons at our latitude, love rarely sparkles, and Nathalie must be a young woman of thirty-seven (and a half). A mother, for all I know. Perhaps of a twelve-year-old daughter herself. Is Nathalie unemployed or satisfied with her role in society? Lost and lonely, or happy in love? A level-headed woman, with a Master's in concessions and oppositions? Does she pour out her feelings of helplessness at mealtimes, or does she bravely think of her daughter's morale as the little one walks through the classroom door?

10

Our "bad students", the ones slated not to *become* anything, never come to school alone. What walks into the classroom is an onion: several layers of school blues – fear, worry, bitterness, anger, dissatisfaction, furious renunciation – wrapped round a shameful past, an ominous present, a future condemned. Look, here they come, their bodies in the process of *becoming* and their families in their rucksacks. The lesson can't really begin until the burden has been laid down and the onion peeled. It's hard to explain, but just one look is often enough, a kind remark, a clear, steady word from a considerate grown-up, to dissolve those blues, lighten those minds and settle those kids comfortably into the present indicative.

Naturally, the benefits are temporary; the onion will layer itself back together outside the classroom, and we'll have to start all over again tomorrow. But that's what teaching is all about: starting over again and again until we reach the critical moment when the teacher can disappear. If we fail to settle our students into the present indicative of our lessons, if our knowledge and taste for using this tense doesn't "take" – in the botanical sense – then these young lives will lurch over and into the potholes of undefined want. Of course, we won't have been the only ones to dig those potholes, nor the only ones ignorant of how to fill them in, but these young men and women will have spent a year or more of their youth sitting right here, in front of us. And a wasted academic year isn't something you can just dismiss: it's eternity in a goldfish bowl.

11

Learning requires the invention of a special kind of tense. The *present tense incarnate*, for example. Here I am, in this class, and I understand, at last. I've got it. My brain is reaching out to the rest of my body: the word is *being made flesh*.

When this isn't the case, when I don't understand anything, I crumble on the spot, I disintegrate as time stands still, I collapse in the dust, and the slightest breath scatters me.

For knowledge to have a chance of being embodied in the present tense of a lesson, we need to stop brandishing the past as something shameful and the future as a punishment.

12

And while we're on the subject, what do they become, those who *become something*?

F. died a few months after retiring. J. threw himself out a window on the eve of his retirement. G. is having a nervous breakdown. Another acquaintance has only just emerged from his. J. F.'s doctors say the onset of his Alzheimer's dates back to his first year of early retirement. P. B.'s doctors likewise. Poor L. cries her eyes out at having been made redundant from the press group where she thought she'd be making the news forever. I still think of P. the cobbler, who died when he couldn't find a buyer for his business. "So my life is worth nothing?" That's what he kept asking. Nobody wanted to buy up his raison d'être. "All that for nothing." Despondency did for him.

This one's a diplomat who'll be retiring in six months' time. What he fears more than anything is having to face himself. He's looking for something to do: consulting for a multinational industrial group? Advising here or there? And that one got to be prime minister. The job he'd dreamt about for thirty years, since his first electoral successes. His wife always encouraged him to go for it. He's a political long-haul lorry driver. He knew the top job in such-and-such a government would be temporary. And dangerous. He knew that the press would make a laughing stock of him at the first opportunity, that he would be the target of choice, even in his own party: Scapegoat Number 1. Chances are, he was familiar with Clemenceau's joke about his own chief of staff: "When I fart, he stinks." (Ah yes, the elegant world of politics. Having to weigh public pronouncements by the milligram makes you all the coarser when you're among "friends".) So, he becomes prime minister. He accepts the perilous short-term contract. He and his wife become battle-hardened. Prime minister for a few years, fine. The few years pass. Predictably, he's out. Prime minister no more. His confidants confirm that he's reeling from the blow: "He's concerned about his future." So much so that a nervous breakdown drags him to the edge of suicide.

What an evil spell is cast by the social roles for which we're raised and educated, and which we go on to play "all our lives", in other words for roughly half our time on this earth. Release us from these roles and we're no longer the same actors.

When a career come to a dramatic end, it evokes a feeling of helplessness comparable, in my view, to that experienced by the tortured teenager who, thinking he has no future, finds it so painful to carry on. Reduced to ourselves, we feel reduced to nothing. To the point where we may even destroy ourselves. This is, at the very least, a flaw in our education.

13

There came a year of particular discontent, when I was miserable and fed up with who I was, and rather keen not to *become* anything. My bedroom window gave on to the *baous* of La Gaude and Saint-Jeannet, two sheer rock faces in the southern Alps, notorious for cutting short the suffering of rejected lovers. One morning, as I was contemplating these cliffs a little too affectionately, there was a knock on my bedroom door. It was my father. He poked his head round and said, "Ah! Daniel, I forgot to mention that suicide is not a good idea."

14

Let us return to my beginnings. Deeply distressed by my theft from the family safe, my mother sought advice from the headmaster of my *collège*. He was an easy-going and perspicacious character, with a reassuring big nose (the students nicknamed him Conk). Judging me to be puny and anxious rather than dangerous, Conk recommended sending me away to school and plenty of fresh air. A high-altitude stint would put the hair back on my chest. A boarding school in the mountains, yes, that was the answer: I would become stronger and more confident while learning the rules of community life. Don't worry, Mrs Pennacchioni, you're the mother of a little dreamer, not of Arsène Lupin, and your dreamer requires a dose of reality. Thus began my first two years as a boarder – starting at the age of twelve – when I only ever saw my family at Christmas, at Easter and during the summer holidays. Subsequently, I was moved to schools where I went home at the weekends.

The question of whether I was "happy" at boarding school is secondary. Let's just say that being a boarder was infinitely more bearable than being a day boy.

It's difficult to explain the advantages of a boarding school to today's parents, who see such places as penal colonies. For them, sending your children away is an act of abandonment. Even daring to suggest a year at boarding school makes you sound like a reactionary monster lobbying for the imprisonment of dunces. There's no point explaining that you survived one yourself, because the argument of a bygone era is immediately put forward: "Yes, but back then kids were used to toughing it out!"

Today, with the invention of parental love, boarding schools are taboo in France, except as a threat, which proves nobody believes they could be part of the solution.

That said . . .

No, I'm not going to set about justifying boarding schools.

No.

Let me describe instead the everyday nightmare of a student who is "failing".

15

Which student? One of those my telephone mothers ring up about, for example, and whom they'd never send to boarding school, not for anything in the world. Let's take a best-case scenario. He's a good kid, loved by his family. He hasn't got it in for anyone, but because he can't make head or tail of anything, he's stopped making an effort and receives school reports in which exhausted teachers give vent to remarks devoid of hope: "Doesn't work", "Hasn't done any assignments", "In freefall" and, more darkly, "What can I say?" (As I write these lines, I have that report, and a few others, in front of me.)

Let's follow our bad student through a typical school day. Exceptionally, he's on time – recently his *carnet de correspondance* has too often noted his tardiness – but his rucksack is nearly empty: text-books, exercise books, essential materials forgotten yet again (on his end-of-term report, his music teacher will write nattily: "Missing a flute".)

Of course his homework hasn't been done. His first class is mathematics, and his problems are among those missing when the register is called. There are three possibilities here: either he didn't do his problems because he was busy with something else (hanging out with his mates; playing a video game behind his locked bedroom door . . .); or he flopped on his bed, and zoned out as a torrent of music roared inside his head; or – and this is the most optimistic hypothesis – he struggled bravely with his problems for an hour or two, but couldn't manage to do them.

In each scenario, not handing in his homework means that our student needs somehow to justify his behaviour to his teacher. The most difficult explanation to serve up in this instance is the simple truth: "Sir, miss, I didn't do my homework because I spent half the night in cyberspace defeating the soldiers of Evil, which, by the way, I exterminated down to the last one, no, really, trust me." "Miss, sir, sorry I didn't do my homework, but yesterday evening I couldn't keep my eyes open, I couldn't even move my little finger, I could barely turn on my M.P.3."

In these examples, the truth involves the inconvenience of a confession – "I didn't do my homework" – which calls for an immediate sanction. Our student would prefer an institutionally more presentable version. For example: "My parents are divorced, and I left my homework round at my dad's when I went back home to Mum's." In other words, a lie. For his part, the teacher often prefers this type of massaged truth to a bald confession that might undermine his own authority. By avoiding a head-on clash, both student and teacher get something out of a diplomatic pas de deux. As for marks, we all know the going rate for homework not handed in: zero.

Things are scarcely different for the student who tried bravely, but without success, to do his homework. He too walks into the classroom, keeper of an uncomfortable truth: "Sir, I spent two hours last night *not doing* your homework. No, no, I didn't do anything else; I sat down at my desk, I got out my exercise book, I read the problem, but for two hours I drew a mathematical blank; I only escaped mental paralysis when I heard my mum calling me for supper. So I didn't do my homework, but I really did spend two hours on it. After supper it was too late, another bout of catalepsy awaited me: my English homework."

"If you paid attention in class, you'd understand your homework assignments!" the teacher might object (and with good reason).

To avoid this kind of public humiliation, our student would prefer a diplomatic presentation of the facts: "I was just reading the essay title when the boiler exploded."

And so on, from morning to night, from subject to subject, from teacher to teacher, from day to day, an exponential lie leading to Truffaut's immortal line: "It's my mother, sir, she's dead!"

After a day spent lying to the educational establishment, the first question our bad student hears on returning home is the time-honoured "Did you have a good day at school?"

"Great."

A new lie.

Which needs cutting with a sliver of truth: "In history, the teacher asked me what happened in 1515; I said Marignan; she was dead impressed!"

(Right, that'll tide me over until tomorrow.)

But tomorrow comes around so fast, and the days repeat themselves, and our student continues the to-and-fro between school and family, and all his mental energy is spent in weaving a subtle network of pseudo-coherence between the lies offered at school and the half-truths served up at home, between explanations furnished and justifications supplied, between portraits of teachers painted for his parents and allusions to family problems whispered into his teachers' ears, always a grain of truth in each, for these people will end up meeting, parents and teachers, it's inevitable, and you've got to bear that in mind, keep on polishing the true life story on which the interview will be based.

The energy mobilized by such mental activity is on an entirely different scale from the effort invested by a good student in a good piece of homework. Our bad student is wearing himself out. He wouldn't have the strength left to work properly even if he wanted to (and he does, from time to time). The fiction in which he's bogged down holds him prisoner *elsewhere*, somewhere between the school he's got to do battle against and his family, which needs reassuring, in an excruciating third dimension where the role allotted to the imagination consists of plugging the countless gaps through which reality might escape in its most fearful guises. A lie discovered: anger on one side, hurt on the other, accusations, sanctions, expulsion perhaps, no escape, helpless guilt, humiliation, morose delectation. *They're right, I'm nothing, nothing, nothing.*

I'm a no-hoper.

Now, in the society in which we live, a teenager convinced his case is hopeless – here at least is something lived experience will have taught us – is a victim.

16

The reasons that teachers and parents choose to disregard these lies, and even to become complicit in them, are too numerous to discuss here. How many daily fibs from four or five classes of thirty-five students each can a teacher legitimately question? Where would I find the time for such enquiries? And anyway, am I an investigator? Should I, in the name of moral education, act in loco parentis? If so, within what parameters? And so on, a litany of questions debated heatedly by teachers and their colleagues.

But there is another reason for a teacher ignoring these lies, a deeply buried reason which, if it were granted an airing, might sound something like this: what this boy personifies is my own professional failure. I'm not getting him to make progress or to do any work, I'm only just about getting him to turn up, and even then all I can be certain of is his physical presence.

As luck would have it, barely has this self-questioning raised its head than it is beaten down by a number of permissible arguments. Okay, so I'm failing this one, but I'm succeeding with a lot of others.

It's hardly my fault if this boy was allowed to move up into this year group. What on earth did my predecessors teach him? Is this just the school's fault? What's happening at home? Do people really imagine that, with my schedule and quotas, I can get him up to speed when he's so far behind?

All these questions lump together the student's past, his family, other teachers and the school itself in such a way that they enable us, with a clear conscience, to write that most common of remarks on a school report: *Lacks basic skills* (a comment I've even seen on a first-year primary-school report, by the way). In other words, a hot potato.

That potato is hottest for the parents. They never stop flipping it from hand to hand. The kid's daily lies wear them out: lies of omission, pure fabrications, overly detailed explanations: "So basically, what happened was . . ."

A fair number of battle-weary parents pretend to believe in these debilitating fables, in order to balance their own mounting anguish with a temporary sense of respite (the grain of truth – Marignan, 1515 – playing out its role as an aspirin tablet), and to keep a lid on the atmosphere at home, so supper doesn't turn into a drama: *not tonight, please, not tonight.* Anything to delay an ordeal that will prove harrowing for all parties; in short, to push back the moment when the end-of-term report arrives and the extent of the academic disaster, no real surprises there, can be measured; although, having kept his eyes trained on the letterbox, the interested party may have tampered with it, and not unsuccessfully . . .

We'll deal with it tomorrow,
we'll deal with it tomorrow . . .

17

One of the most memorable stories of adults being complicit in a child's lie involves the mishap that befell the brother of my friend B. He must have been twelve or thirteen at the time . . . Dreading a maths test, he asks his best friend to show him where the appendix is situated in the human body. He then collapses, simulating an attack of appendicitis. The head teacher pretends to believe him, sends him home, if only to be shot of him. At which point his parents, under no illusions – it's not the first time he's pulled this sort of stunt – drive him to a nearby clinic, where, to everyone's surprise, he is operated on immediately. After the operation, the surgeon appears carrying a jar containing a long, bleeding thingummyjig and declares, his innocent face alight: "It was just as well I operated; we've avoided peritonitis by a whisker!"

For societies too are built on shared lies.

Here's a more recent story: N., head of a Parisian *lycée,* is on the lookout for absenteeism. She takes the register in her final-year classes.

She has her eye on a regular offender whom she's threatened to exclude the next time he's absent without explanation. The boy is absent again; it's a case of once too often. N. immediately rings the family. The mother apologizes and confirms that her son really is sick, bedridden, burning up with fever, and also assures N. that she was just about to inform the *lycée*. N. hangs up, satisfied; all is in order. Except for the fact that she runs into the boy on her way back to her office. He was in the lavatory while she was taking the register.

18

By limiting the comings and goings between school and family, boarding has the advantage of settling our student into two distinct time zones: school from Monday morning to Friday evening, family at the weekend. One group of interlocutors for five working days, the other for two days of holiday (back in with a proper chance of being days off). Academic reality on the one hand, the reality of family life on the other. Being able to go to sleep without having to reassure parents with a daily lie, waking up without having to fashion excuses for work not done, since it was completed during study period the evening before with, best-case scenario, the help of a supervisor or teacher. In short, a calmer state of mind, reclaimed energy that has some chance of being channelled into schoolwork. Enough to propel the dunce to the top of the class? An opportunity, at least, to live in the present. And it's in being conscious of the present, not fleeing from it, that the individual forms himself.

Here ends my eulogy on the advantages of boarding.

Ah, sorry, at the risk of terrorizing everybody, I'd like to add, since I used to teach in a boarding school myself, that the best boarding schools are those where the teachers also board. Always on call, in case of emergency.

19

It's worth noting that, although boarding schools have had a very bad press over the past twenty years in France, three of the biggest blockbusters and bestsellers among young people during the same period were *Dead Poets Society*, the Harry Potter books and *Les Choristes*. All three set in boarding schools, and three rather archaic boarding schools at that: sinister buildings, dusty professors – even corporal punishment, in *Les Choristes*.

It would be interesting to analyse the success among young viewers of *Dead Poets Society*, a film almost universally panned by critics and staff rooms alike as dumbed down, complacent, old-fashioned, silly, sentimental, cinematically and intellectually impoverished, all charges it would be difficult to refute . . . And yet, hordes of *lycée* students rushed off to see it and came home glowing. To assume they were bewitched by the film's faults is to hold an entire generation in extremely low esteem.

Take John Keating's anachronisms, for example, which didn't escape my students (neither did his bad faith):

"Keating's not entirely 'honest', sir, with his *carpe diem*; the way he talks about it, you'd think we were still in the sixteenth century; but back then, in the sixteenth century, people died much younger than they do today."

"I mean it's disgusting, at the beginning, this guy who makes out he's so open-minded and then he gets them to rip up their textbooks . . . Why not burn all the books he doesn't like while he's at it? I'd have refused, if it'd been me."

Apart from those details, my students "loved" the film. All of them, boys and girls alike, could identify with those young Americans in the late '50s who in fact were about as close to my students (both socially and culturally) as Martians. They were all crazy about Robin Williams (whereas adults found him completely over the top). For my students, his Keating personified human warmth and professional devotion: a passion for the subjects he taught and a total commitment to his students, buoyed up by the dynamism of an indefatigable sports coach. The closed world of boarding school made his lessons seem more intense, conferring a dramatic intimacy that promoted young viewers to the rank of fully fledged students. Keating's lessons seemed a rite of passage intended for them and them alone. Those lessons were none of the family's business. Or the teachers' business either, come to that. Cutting to the chase, one of my students said: "Big deal, so teachers don't like it. But it's our film, not yours!"

Which is exactly what most of the teachers in question must have thought twenty years earlier when, as students themselves, they celebrated the 1969 *Palme D'Or* winner at the Cannes Film Festival. *If* was another story about a boarding school; it depicted the most brilliant students, in a quintessentially British establishment, storming their school from the rooftops, machine-gunning and mortar-bombing their parents, a bishop and the teachers assembled for prize-giving. Adult spectators were scandalized, which is as it should have been; university students and *lycéens* were of course overjoyed: it's our film, not theirs.

Apparently, times had changed.

So it occurred to me that a study comparing films about school would reveal a great deal about the societies that had produced them. From *Zéro de conduite* by Jean Vigo (1933) to *Dead Poets Society* via *Les Disparus de Saint-Agil* by Christian-Jaque (1939), *La Cage aux Rossignols* by Jean Dreville (1944, the precursor to *Les Choristes*), *Blackboard Jungle* by Richard Brooks (1955), Truffaut's *Les Quatre cent coups* (1959), *The First Teacher* by Andrei Konchalovsky (1965), *The Teacher* by Zurlini

(1972), to which we can add *Il Portaborse* by Daniele Luchette (1991), *The Blackboard* by the Iranian filmmaker Samira Makhmalbaf (2000), *L'Esquive* by Abdellatif Kechiche (2002) and a few dozen others.

My comparative study never progressed beyond an idea; over to anyone who's interested, if it hasn't been done already. A good excuse for a retrospective, at any rate. Given that most of these films have been box-office hits, we could draw a lesson or two from them, including this: since Rabelais, each Gargantuan generation has experienced a juvenile horror of Holofernes and a need for Poncrates. In other words, there's a constantly renewed urge to shape oneself in opposition to the current climate and prevailing mindset, as well as a desire to flourish in the shadow – or rather the light – of a teacher thought to be exemplary.

20

Back to the question of *becoming*.

February 1959, September 1969. Ten years had gone by between the calamitous letter I had written to my mother and the one my father had sent to his son the *teacher*.

Ten years in which I *became* someone.

To what can we ascribe this transformation from dunce into teacher?

And, incidentally, that of illiterate student into novelist?

It's the first question one might ask.

How did I *become*?

It's very tempting not to reply. By arguing, for example, that the process of maturation, whether for human beings or for oranges, defies explanation. At what point does the most rebellious teenager touch down on the ground of social reality? When does he decide to play, if only a little, that game? Is it purely a case of making the decision to do so? What role does evolution play, the chemistry of cells, the meshing of neural networks? So many questions helping to avoid the subject.

"If what you write about your own experience as a dunce is true," someone might object, "your transformation into a teacher is some mystery!"

In other words, they don't believe me. Which is the dunce's lot: never to be believed. While a dunce, he stands accused of disguising his depraved laziness with convenient complaints: "Stop making excuses and do some work!" When he does well as an adult, he is suspected of showing off: "You used to be a dunce? Come off it, you're just blowing your own horn!" The dunce's cap is gladly worn looking back. It's a covetable accessory in today's society. It distinguishes you from those whose only merit was to follow the clearly signposted paths of learning. High society is teeming with yesterday's heroic dunces. They can be heard, these shrewd operators, at literary gatherings, over the airwaves, trumpeting their academic setbacks as great feats of resistance. Personally, I don't believe them unless I detect actual pain behind their words. For although people sometimes recover from being dunces, the wounds never heal completely. A childhood like that is no laughing matter, nor is remembering it. It's not something to be proud of. The former asthmatic doesn't boast of having felt he was about to suffocate to death a thousand times. That said, the last thing the dunce who got over it wants is for people to pity him; he wants to forget about it, that's all, not to have to think about the shame any more. He knows, deep down, that he could so easily not have got over it. After all, those dunces lost to history are in the majority. I've always felt like someone who has been lucky to survive.

So what happened to me in the course of those ten years?

How did I come through?

A preliminary remark: adults and children, as we know, do not share the same perception of time. Ten years is nothing in the eyes of an adult who calculates his existence in decades. Ten years pass in a flash when you're fifty. And that same sense of speed whets the anxiety of mothers for the futures of their sons. He'll be taking his *bac* in five years, my goodness, it might as well be tomorrow. How can my little one change so dramatically in such a short time? Whereas, for the little one, each of those years is worth a thousand; for him, his future means the next few days. So talking to him about what lies ahead is tantamount to asking him to measure infinity with a decimetre. The verb "to become" paralyses him, primarily because it expresses adult worry or disapproval. The future means a worse version of myself – crudely speaking, this was how I translated my teachers' assertion that I would come to nothing. As I listened to them, I didn't factor time into the equation at all, I just believed what they told me: always a cretin, never a success, "always" and "never" being the two units of time measurement that wounded pride makes available to the dunce.

Time . . . I didn't realize I would have to age in order to acquire a logarithmic sense of its passing. (I was, for that matter, completely ignorant when it came to logarithms, their tables, their functions, their scales and beguiling curves . . .) Once I became a teacher, I instinctively knew it was pointless brandishing the future at my worst students. Sufficient unto the day is the evil thereof, and unto each lesson in that day, provided we are fully present and working together.

As a child, I was ignorant of all this. I had only to set foot inside a classroom to find myself making a swift exit. The master's stare from on high, like one of those beams from a flying saucer, would no sooner eject me from my chair than it dispatched me somewhere else. Where, exactly? Into his head. The teacher's head. I was beamed into his flying-saucer laboratory. There, the full extent of my hopelessness was measured before the next stare spat me back out, like so much detritus. And so I rolled around in a field of manure where I couldn't understand what was being taught or what the school expected from me, since I'd been labelled unfit for purpose. This verdict at least offered me the compensation of laziness: why kill yourself trying when, as far as the powers that be are concerned, the game's up anyway? Clearly, I was developing an aptitude for casuistry. (As a teacher, I quickly spotted this cast of mind among my own dunces.)

Then along came my first saviour.

A French teacher.

When I was fourteen.

Who spotted me for what I was: a sincere and joyously suicidal storyteller.

No doubt amazed by my increasingly inventive excuses as to why I hadn't done my revision or my homework, he decided to excuse me from essays and commission a novel instead. A novel I was to write in a single term, at the rate of a chapter a week. On a subject of my own choosing, but with the proviso that I deliver my instalments without spelling mistakes, in order to "raise the tone" of the teacher's criticism. (I remember that phrase even though I've long forgotten the subject of the novel.) This teacher, an extremely elderly man, dedicated the last years of his life to us, rounding out his retirement in that ultra-private school in the suburbs north of Paris. An old gentleman of old-fashioned distinction who had spotted the *narrator* in me. Despite my severe spelling problems, he'd clearly realized that the only way to get through to me was via narrative. I wrote that novel with enthusiasm. I corrected each word scrupulously with the help of a dictionary (which, to this day, I'm never without), and I delivered my chapters as punctually as a professional writer submitting in instalments. I expect it was a gloomy narrative, since I was strongly influenced at the time by Thomas Hardy, whose novels progress from misunderstanding to catastrophe, and from catastrophe to irreparable tragedy, thereby thrilling my taste for *fate*: nothing doing from the outset, was my take on things.

I don't think I made substantial progress in any subject that year, but, for the first time in my experience, a teacher had accorded me some kind of status; I existed academically, as an individual with a path to follow, and as someone who kept going to the end.

I feel boundless gratitude towards my benefactor, of course, and although the old man was rather aloof, he became privy to my secret reading sessions.

"Well, Pennacchioni, what are you reading at the moment?"

For there was reading.

I didn't realize, then, that reading would save me.

At the time, being able to read wasn't considered the absurd prowess it is today. Thought of as a waste of time, as harmful to schoolwork, the reading of novels was forbidden during study periods. Hence my vocation as a clandestine reader: novels covered to give them the appearance of textbooks, books hidden all over the place, nocturnal reading by torchlight, excuses from P.E. classes, anything to find myself alone with books. Boarding school gave me the taste for reading. I needed to create a world of my own there, and that was where books came in. At home, I had mostly watched other people read: my father in his armchair smoking his pipe, under the light-cone of a lamp, distractedly running his ring finger down the impeccable parting of his hair, legs crossed, a book open on his knees; Bernard, in our bedroom, curled up on his side, right hand propping up his head . . . a sense of well-being was implied by these poses. It was the reader's physicality that got me into reading. Perhaps in the beginning, I only read in order to reproduce those postures and to explore others. And as I read, I would settle down into a state of physical happiness that persists to this day. What did I read? Andersen's fairy tales, because I identified with the Ugly Duckling; Alexandre Dumas for the sword action, the horses and the heartbreak. And Selma Lagerlöf, the magnificent *Gösta Berling*, that splendid drunken pastor, banished by his bishop, whose indefatigable companion in adventure I became, along with Ekeby's other cavalrymen. *War and Peace*, given to me by Bernard when I was thirteen, I think, a love story at first reading (that reduces the novel to a hundred pages), a Napoleonic epic at fourteen, on second reading – Austerlitz, Borodino, the fire of Moscow, the Russian retreat (I drew a huge fresco of the Battle of Austerlitz, in which the little stick-men of my clandestine writing slaughtered each other) – two or three hundred more pages.

A new reading at fifteen, the friendship of Pierre Bezukhov (another Ugly Duckling, but one who understood more than people thought he did), and finally the whole novel, in one of my final years at school, for Russia, for the character of Kutuzov, for Clausewitz, for the agrarian reforms, for Tolstoy. Naturally there was Dickens – Oliver Twist needed me – Emily Brontë, who looked to me for moral support, Stevenson, Jack London, Oscar Wilde and my first readings of Dostoevsky – *The Gambler*, of course (when it comes to Dostoevsky, I don't know why, but everybody always starts with *The Gambler*). So went my reading, according to what I could find in the library at home, and then there was *Tintin*, of course, and *Spirou*, as well as the *Signes de Piste* imprint and the *Bob Morane* series that were all the rage at the time. The chief criterion I looked for in the novels I took back with me to *collège* was their not being on the syllabus. Nobody could quiz me about them. Nobody would read them over my shoulder; we kept our own company, the authors and I. What I didn't realize, as I read, was that I was cultivating my own tastes, that an appetite was being awakened that would survive long after I had forgotten about those particular books.

These youthful readings opened four doors on to the world, four books that couldn't have been more different, but which wove within me, for reasons that remain mysterious, an intimate sense of affiliation: *Dangerous Liaisons*, *Against the Grain*, *Mythologies* by Roland Barthes and Perec's *Things*.

I wasn't a refined reader. With all due respect to Flaubert, I read like Emma Bovary when I was fifteen, purely to satisfy my cravings, which, luckily, proved insatiable. Nor did I gain any immediate academic advantage from this kind of reading. And, contrary to received wisdom, those thousands of pages swallowed – and very quickly forgotten – didn't improve my spelling, which remains unsteady today (hence my omnipresent dictionaries). No, what provisionally improved my mistakes (the fact that it was provisional made it definitively possible) was that novel ordered up by the teacher who refused to lower his standards by allowing spelling mistakes. I *owed* him a flawless manuscript. In short, he was a pedagogical genius. For me alone, perhaps, and perhaps only in that instance, but a genius nonetheless.

I encountered three other geniuses from the time I was fourteen until my repeated final year, three other saviours of whom more later: a mathematics teacher who *was* mathematics, a staggeringly good history teacher who could bring history to life like nobody else, and a philosophy teacher to whom my ongoing admiration came as a surprise since he has no recollection of me (he wrote to tell me so); this only serves to increase my opinion of him, since he stirred my mind when I owed nothing to his esteem and everything to his art. These four masters saved me from myself. Were they too late? Would I have followed them so faithfully if they had been my primary-school teachers? Would I have happier childhood memories? Whatever the whys and wherefores, they were my happy surprises. Were they the revelation for other students that they were for me? A valid question, since temperament plays its part in pedagogy. When I happen to meet a former student who professes to have enjoyed the hours spent in my class, I tell myself that at that same moment, walking by on another pavement, there may be someone else whose interest I extinguished.

Another element of my transformation was the eruption of love into my alleged unworthiness. Love! For the kind of teenager I thought I was, this was unimaginable. The statistics, however, pointed to it being likely if not inevitable. (Surely not! Just think: capable of inspiring love, me? And in whom?) Love manifested itself for the first time in the form of a touching holiday encounter, expressed itself in copious letter-writing, and was broken off by mutual agreement in the name of youth and geographical distance. The following summer, having had my heart broken by this semi-platonic passion, I took a job as a ship's boy on board a cargo ship, one of the last Liberty ships still working the Atlantic, and I hurled a bundle of letters into the sea, to make the sharks snigger. I had to wait two years for another love to become the first, by dint of the importance that actions confer on words in this domain. A different kind of incarnation, which revolutionized my life and signed my death warrant as a dunce. A woman loved me! For the first time in my life, my own name rang in my ears. A woman was calling me by my name. I existed in the eyes of a woman, in her heart, in her hands, even in her memories – her first glance the morning after made that clear. Chosen out of all the others! Me! Her favourite! Me! By her! (An *hypokhâgne* student, no less, preparing for the competitive entry exam to the E.N.S., when I was about to retake my final year at school.) My barriers burst: all those books I'd read night after night, those thousands of pages for the most part erased from my memory, all that understanding stockpiled without anybody – let alone myself – realizing it, buried under so many layers of oblivion, renunciation and self-denigration, that magma of words bubbling with ideas, and feelings, and every kind of knowledge suddenly exploded the crust of infamy and rushed inside my brain, which resembled an infinitely star-filled firmament. I was buzzing, as today's happy folk might put it. I loved and was loved. How could so much impatient ardour induce such calm and certainty? What confidence was unexpectedly placed in me! And what confidence I suddenly had in myself. For the few years that happiness lasted, there was no question of playing the fool. Of working twice as hard, yes. After my *bac*, I knocked off in less time than it takes to say them, a bachelor's degree in French Language and Literature followed by an M.A., my first novel, whole notebooks of aphorisms which I earnestly called my Laconiques, and countless essays, some of which were destined for my girlfriend's girlfriends, who sought out my ideas on this or that point of history, literature or philosophy. While I was at it I even treated myself to the luxury of a place at the *hypokhâgne*, but I left in order to write that famous first novel. To liberate my pen, to fly with my own wings, in my own sky. I didn't want anything else. As long as my girlfriend loved me.

When my father made his joke about the revolution necessary for me to get my degree and the risk of global conflict if I attempted the *agrégation*, I laughed heartily and replied no, not at all, it hadn't taken a revolution, Dad, it had taken love, goddammit! Love that had lasted for three years. She and I had made that revolution, in bed. As for those teaching exams, forget it, I didn't like lotteries. So, no *agreg*, and no *Capès* either. I'd lost enough time on qualifications. An M.A. and *basta*: the minimum required for teaching. A small-time teacher, Dad. In small establishments, if that's the way it had to be. Returning to the scene of the crime. Looking after the kids who fell into the dustbin in Djibouti. Looking after them with a clear memory of what I had once been. And for the rest, literature! The novel. Teaching and the novel. Reading, writing, teaching!

My wake-up call also owes much to the tenacity of my seemingly distant father. Never discouraged by my despondency, he knew how to fend off my attempts at escape: my vehement petitioning, for example, when I was fourteen, to get him to enrol me in the army. We laughed about it a great deal twenty years later, when, released after national service, I handed over my military record which read, *Rank upon Discharge: Private (second-class).*

"Private second-class, eh? It's just as I thought: you're ill-suited to obedience and have no taste for leadership."

There was also my old friend Jean Rolin, philosophy teacher and father of Nicolas, Jeanne and Jean-Paul, my friends in adolescence. Each time I failed the *bac*, Jean would take me out to an excellent restaurant in order to convince me, once again, that everybody develops at their own pace and that I was just a slow developer. Jean, my dear Jean, may these pages – true to form, so late in the day – make you smile, in your philosophers' paradise.

21

In short, we *become.*

But we don't change that much. We make do with what we are.

So here I am at the end of Part II, plagued by doubts. Doubts as to the point of this book, doubts about my ability to write it, self-doubt plain and simple, doubts that will blossom into sarcastic reflections on my work as a whole, on my entire life, for that matter . . . Proliferating doubts . . . Such crises of confidence aren't uncommon. They may well be the legacy of my time as a dunce, but I can never get used to them. One always doubts as if for the first time, and my capacity for doubt is devastating. It emphasizes my natural inclination. I'm putting up a fight, but with each passing day I'm turning back into that bad student I've been trying to describe to you. His symptoms are dead ringers for what I experienced as a thirteen-year-old: daydreaming, procrastination, inability to focus, hypochondria, restlessness, morose delectation, mood shifts, whingeing and, to top it all, a blank in front of my computer screen, just as, in the old days, in front of my homework, or the test I had to revise for . . . *Here I am,* sniggers the dunce I once was.

I look up. My gaze wanders over the southern Vercors. Not a house to be seen. Or a road. Or a person. Stony fields bordered by low mountains, clumps of beech trees unfurling here and there like silent plumes. Over all this emptiness looms a threatening sky. My God, how I love this landscape. Deep down, one of my greatest joys is to have given myself the exile that, as a child, I demanded from my parents . . . The horizon, on this side of which no-one is accountable to anyone. (Except for that little rabbit down there, who'll have to answer to that buzzard . . .) In the desert, it's not the Devil who tempts but the desert itself: the natural temptation of all abandonment.

Right, that's enough of that,
stop making such a palaver out of nothing:
back to work.

22

Back to work. Line after line I carry on *becoming*, as this book develops.

We *become*.

One after another, we *become*.

It rarely happens the way we'd expected it might, but one thing is for sure: we become someone.

Last week, as I was leaving a cinema, a little girl, nine or ten years old, chased after me in the street. Catching up with me, all breathless: "Mister, mister . . . !"

What is it? Have I left my umbrella behind at the fleapit? All smiles, the little girl points to a man watching us from the other side of the road.

"That's my grandfather!"

Grandfather sketches an embarrassed wave.

"He's too shy to say hello, but you used to be his teacher . . ."

". . ."

Hell's bells! Her grandfather? I was her grandfather's teacher!

So you see, we do *become*.

". . ."

You part company with a thirteen-year-old kid who's a no-hoper, no-hoper, no-hoper, or that's her opinion ("I was such a no-hoper!"), and twenty years later a radiant young woman calls out to you from a café terrace in Ajaccio: "Mr Pennacchioni, '*Ne touchez pas l'épaule du cavalier qui passe!*'"

You stop, you turn around, the young woman smiles, and you recite that verse of *L'Allée*, the poem by Supervielle, back at her:

Be careful not to touch the shoulder
of the passing horseman.
He would turn around
and it would be night time,
a starless night, no curve or cloud.

She bursts out laughing, and asks:

So what would become of
all that is the sky
the moon and her journey
the noise of the sun?

And you answer the child who has reappeared in the woman's smile, the rebellious child to whom you taught this poem long ago:

Ah, you must wait
until a second horseman
as powerful as the first,
consents to come your way.

In Paris, I'm chatting with some friends in a café. A man points at me from a neighbouring table, and stares hard. I raise my eyebrows and nod at him: what does he want? He promptly addresses me by a name other than my own: "Don Segundo Sombra!"

And in so doing, causes me to take a dizzying leap back in time:

"*You*, I taught you in 1982!"

"Spot on. You read *Don Segundo Sombra* to us, by Ricardo Güiraldes."

I can never remember the names of the students I bump into, or indeed their faces, but from the first verse, the first title, the first reference to a specific lesson, something resurfaces of the teenager who didn't want to read or the little girl who claimed she didn't understand a single word; they become as familiar to me again as Supervielle's verses or Segundo Sombra's name, which, and I've no idea why, have not been eroded by time. They are, at one and the same moment, that frightened child and this young fashion designer, that mulish boy and this flight captain with his nose in a book high above the oceans, having switched his aircraft on to automatic pilot.

With each encounter, I note that a life has flourished as unpredictably as a cloud formation.

But be careful, don't flatter yourself that these destinies owe so much to your influence as a teacher. I check the time on my pocket watch, which my wife, Minne, gave me for a birthday long ago, and which I'm never without. A fob watch like this, with its double case, is known as a savonnette. I glance at my savonnette and all of a sudden it's fifteen years ago, Lycée H., Room F, where I'm busy invigilating for sixty students, cocooned in the silence of their futures. Each is intent on covering his exam paper in more black ink than the next person, apart from Emmanuel, to my right, near the window, three or four rows away from the podium. Nose in the air, blank sheet of paper, that's Emmanuel. Our eyes meet. My expression is unequivocal: What's going on? Blank sheet? You *are* going to knuckle down, aren't you? Emmanuel indicates he'd like to speak to me. He was a student of mine two years previously. Smart, quick, lazy, inventive, funny and determined. And, right now, in possession of a conspicuously blank answer paper. I go over to him, time to give him a good shaking up, but he pre-empts my warning shot by saying, with a sigh: "You've no idea how this bores the shit out of me, sir!"

What can you do with a student like that? Shoot him there and then? I'm unsure where we're heading, and even though it's hardly the time or the place, I ask him: "Might we know what *does* interest you?"

"This," he answers, handing back my savonnette, which he's pinched off me without my noticing.

"And that," he adds, giving me back my pen.

"A pickpocket? You want to become a pickpocket?"

"A magician, sir."

Which is exactly what he became, still is, and he's famous too, not that I had any part in it.

Yes, life-plans sometimes do pan out, vocations are sometimes followed, the future does sometimes honour its appointments. A friend tells me there's a surprise in store at the restaurant to which he's taking me for a meal. I go. It really is a surprise. It's Rémi, the establishment's chef. Impressive to his full height of 1.8 metres, in his white chef's toque. I don't recognize him at first, but he refreshes my memory by putting in front of me a piece of his homework, corrected by me twenty-five years ago. 13/20. Essay title: "Describe Yourself at Forty". The forty-year-old man standing in front of me, smiling and vaguely intimidated by seeing his old teacher, is the spitting image of the essay description: a restaurant chef whose kitchens he compared to the engine room of an ocean liner. His teacher had noted his appreciation, in red, and had expressed his desire to sit at a table in that restaurant one day . . .

Although I'm no longer a teacher, it's in situations like these that I don't regret having *become* one.

We grow up, we *become*, every single one of us, and sometimes we cross paths with others who have *become*. Take Isabelle, whom I met in a theatre last week. She is, as she approaches forty, astonishingly like the sixteen-year-old kid who used to be my student . . . She ended up in my class, having been expelled twice. ("My second expulsion in three years, not bad, eh!") Now a speech therapist with a sensible smile.

Like the others, she asks me: "Do you remember What's-Her-Name? And What's-His-Name? And that other guy?"

Alas, dear students, my wretched memory still refuses to store proper nouns. Their capital letters continue to act as barriers. It only takes the summer holidays for me to forget most of your names, so imagine what it's like with the passing years. There's a sort of permanent siphoning off from my brain, a process which discards, along with your names, the names of the writers I read, the titles of their books or of the films I see, the towns I pass through, the itineraries I follow, the wines I drink . . . Which doesn't mean that you sink into oblivion. Seeing you again for five minutes is all it takes for Rémi's confident face, Nadia's hearty laugh, Emmanuel's mischief, Christian's thoughtfulness, Axelle's liveliness and Arthur's cast-iron humour to resuscitate the student in this man or that woman kind enough to recognize their teacher. I can in fact reveal that your memory has always been speedier and more reliable than mine, even when we were learning those weekly texts together, the ones we had to be able to recite to one another at any given point in the year. An average annual harvest of thirty texts of all kinds, about which Isabelle proudly declares: "I haven't forgotten a single one, sir!"

"You must have had your favourites . . ."

"Yes, here's one you told us we'd be mature enough to understand in sixty years' time."

And she recites the extract in question, which, as it happens, lands in just the right place to conclude this chapter about *becoming*:

> My grandfather used to say: "Life is astoundingly short. To me, looking back over it, life seems so foreshortened that I scarcely understand, for instance, how a young man can decide to ride over to the next village without being afraid that – not to mention accidents – even the span of a normal happy life may fall far short of the time needed for such a journey."

In a gesture of reverence, Isabelle names the author: Franz Kafka. And adds: "In your favourite translation, by Vialatte."

III

Y = There,
or the Present Incarnate

I'll never get there

I

"I'll never get there, sir."

"Sorry?"

"I'll never get there!"

"Where do you want to go?"

"Nowhere! I don't want to go anywhere!"

"So why are you frightened of not getting there?"

"That's not what I mean!"

"What *do* you mean?"

"I'll never get there, that's all!"

"Write that on the board: 'I'll never get there'."

Ill never get their.

"You've made a mistake with *their.* What you've written is the possessive pronoun; I'll explain in a moment. Please correct it. *There,* in this instance, has two *e*'s. And *I'll* is written *i* apostrophe *ll.*"

I'll never get there.

"Good. So what's this *there*, in your opinion?"

"Dunno."

"What does it mean?"

"Dunno."

"Well, we've really got to find out what it means, because it's this *there* that's frightening you."

"I'm not frightened."

"You're not?"

"No."

"You're not frightened of not getting there?"

"I don't give a toss."

"I beg your pardon?"

"Whatever. I'm not bothered about it."

"You're not bothered about not getting there?"

"I'm not bothered, end of."

"Can you write that on the board?"

"What, 'I'm not bothered about it'?"

"Yes."

Im not bovered about it.

"*I* apostrophe *m.* And you might like to replace that *v* with a *th* – that's more like it."

I'm not bothered about it.

"Good. What about this *it*, while we're at it, what is this *it*?"

". . ."

"This *it*, what is it?"

"Dunno, do I . . . ? It's – *all that*!"

"*All that*? Meaning what?"

"Everything that bugs me!"

2

That year, beginning with our very first lessons together, my students and I attacked *there* and *it*, as well as *everything*. Via these words we mounted our assault on the stronghold of grammar. If we wanted to settle into the present indicative of our lessons, we needed to get to grips with these mysterious agents of disembodiment. Top priority! So we hunted hazy pronouns. Those enigmatic words showed up like so many abscesses to be drained.

There came first, this famous *there* to which we never get. Let's skip its classification as an adverbial pronoun, since that sounds like Chinese to a French student hearing it for the first time; let's cut open its belly and scoop out all the possible meanings; we'll stick a grammatical label on it later, when we stitch it back up again, its guts having been catalogued and reinserted. Grammarians accord *there* an imprecise value. Well, *we* will be precise, *we* will be specific!

In that particular year, for that particular boy who shouted and swore like a trooper, *there* was the bitter memory of a maths problem he couldn't get his head round. It had triggered an outburst: biro hurled to the floor, exercise book slammed shut (look, I just don't get *it*, I don't give a toss about *it*, *it* bugs me etc.), student sent out of the classroom only to explode again in the next lesson, with me, in French, where he came crashing up against another difficulty, with grammar this time, but which reminded him cruelly of the previous problem – the *y* in algebra now in the guise of the French word *y*, meaning "*there*" . . .

Je n'y arriverai jamais . . .

"I'll never get there, I'm telling you. It just wasn't meant to be, sir, school and me!"

(That's a national debate, my friend, soon to be a century old. As to whether school was meant for you or you for school, you have no idea how much blood is spilled over that subject in educational high places.)

"Three years ago, did you think you would ever make it this far?"

"Not really, no. They even wanted to keep me back a year at primary school."

"But here you are, more than halfway through *collège*. You *got there*."

(By dint of seniority, perhaps, and in a sorry state, I'll grant you; willingly or not, that's your business; appropriately or not, that's for higher-ups to debate; but the fact is you got *here*, and we're all *here* with you, and now that we're all *here*, we're going to spend the year *here*, we're going to work on *it* together and do our best to sort a few things out, starting with the most pressing matters: the fear of not getting *there*, the temptation not to be bothered about *it*, the obsession with labelling everything else as "*all that*". How many people in this city are frightened of not getting *there*, and think they're not bothered about *it* . . . But of course they're bothered about *it*; they act out, they get depressed, they go off the rails, they shout, they explode, their game is frightening people, but if there's anything they most definitely are bothered about, it's *there* and *it*, which are ruining their lives, not to mention all that other stuff that's bugging them.)

"What's the point?"

"What's the point, indeed? In fact, let's have a good hard look at this *point*, shall we? Because it's starting to get on my nerves, the way you keep asking: what's the point, what's the point . . . ? Let's see: what *point*, for example, do those words have in your mouth, right now?"

So that year, we cut open the bellies of *there* and *it*, and of *all* and *that*. Each time they surfaced, we tried to discover what these depressing words were hiding. They were like infinitely expandable wineskins supplying ballast to ancient ships, and we emptied them the way one bails out a capsizing dinghy, examining closely what got thrown overboard:

First up, *there* was a maths problem that sparked things off.

Next, *there* was a grammatical problem that got the fire going again. ("Grammar bugs me even more than maths, sir!")

And so on. *There*'s English, which is impossible to understand;

there's design and technology, which bugs him along with everything else (ten years later it'll *mash his brain*, and ten years after that it'll be – *like – totally minging*); *there* are all those grown-ups expecting him to achieve the impossible. In short, *there are* all the different aspects of his education.

Hence the appearance of *it*, as in *not being bothered about it.* (Or not giving a toss about it, or a damn about it, or a shit about it, or indeed *not giving a flying f**k about it* – it's all about testing the resilience of teachers' ears.)

It's the record of his daily failures.

It's grown-ups' opinion of him.

It's his feeling of humiliation, which he converts into hatred for his teachers and contempt for good students . . .

Hence his refusal to try to understand the enormity of *that* – what's the point? – and his permanent desire to be somewhere else, to be doing something else, no matter where, no matter what.

Their scrupulous dissection of *there* revealed the image these students had of themselves: no-hopers lost in an absurd universe, choosing not to give a damn since they couldn't imagine a future for themselves.

"Not even in our dreams, sir!"

No future.

There's the impenetrable hereafter.

Except that if you can't picture a future for yourself, then you can't settle in the present either. You're sitting on your chair but you're somewhere else, prisoner in some dreadful limbo, a place where time stands still, a kind of perpetuity, and you feel as if you're being tortured, and you want to make somebody pay for this, it doesn't matter who, as long as someone does.

Hence the teacher in me decided to use parsing to bring them *here, now*, in order to experience the singular thrill of understanding the purpose of adverbial pronouns, essential words we use a thousand times a day without having to think about it. It's a complete waste of energy, when faced with this angry student, to get lost in moral or psychological arguments; this is not a time for debate but for action.

Once *there* and *it* had been lifted out and cleaned up, we duly labelled them. As two adverbial pronouns, extremely useful when it comes to sidestepping prickly questions. We compared them to cellars of language, these pronouns, and to inaccessible attics, to a suitcase you never open, to a parcel forgotten in a left-luggage locker whose key you've lost.

"A hideout, sir, it's a bloody hideout!"

And not such a good one, as it happens. We think we're hiding inside it only to discover that the hideout is consuming us. Swallowed up by *there* and *it*, we don't know who we are any more.

3

Grammatical wrongs are cured with grammar, spelling mistakes with spelling practice, fear of reading with reading, not understanding a text by immersing yourself in it, habitual non-thinking by the calm reinforcement of reasoning confined to what we are doing here, now, in this classroom, during this lesson, for as long as we remain *here.*

I derived this conviction from my own schooling. I was lectured at a great deal; people often tried to reason with me, and with the best of intentions, for there is no lack of kindness among teachers. The head of the *collège* to which my domestic burglary got me sent was one such example. A sailor, a former sea captain versed in the patience of oceans, he was also a father and the attentive husband of a wife said to suffer from a mysterious illness. A man busy both with his own family and with running this boarding school where there was no shortage of cases like mine. And yet how many hours did he spend trying to convince me that I wasn't the idiot I claimed to be, that my dreams of African exile were mere escapism, that all I had to do was apply myself and my whinging would stop getting the better of my ability? I thought it very good of him to show some interest when I knew he had so many worries of his own, and I promised to pull myself together, yes, right you are, on the double. But as soon as I was back in a maths lesson, or bent over my biology homework during evening study period, that unshakeable confidence would evaporate. The point being that we didn't talk about algebra, my headmaster and I, or about photosynthesis, but about willingness, about concentration; we talked about me, a version of me open to the notion of making progress; the head was convinced I could make progress if only I would put my mind to it. This version of me, buoyant with hope, swore to make an effort, to stop lying to himself; but alas, ten minutes later, confronted with algebra, that other me deflated like a punctured balloon, and in evening study period, faced with the inexplicable taste that plants have for carbon dioxide via that strange substance known as chlorophyll, my only option was to give up. I turned back into the familiar fool who would never understand anything, because he *never had done.*

This misadventure of mine, repeated so many times, convinced me that I had to speak to my students in the language of the subject I was teaching them. Fear of grammar? Let's tackle grammar. No appetite for literature? Let's read! For, strange as it might seem, dear students, you are full of the subjects we teach you. Indeed, you are the subject matter of all subject matters. Unhappy at school? Perhaps. Knocked sideways by life? Some of you, yes. But for me, made of words, every single one of you, woven from grammar, bursting with points of view, even the most silent among you or those least armed with vocabulary, haunted by your descriptions of the world; in short, you are full of literature, each and every one of you. I beg you to believe this.

4

The best-intended psychological interventions may come to nothing. A class of seventeen-year-olds. Jocelyne is in tears, the lesson can't begin. Nothing blocks knowledge better than the blues. You can silence laughter with a single look, but tears . . .

"Has anybody got a funny story they can tell? We've got to make Jocelyne laugh so that we can begin. Wrack your brains. A *very* funny story. Three minutes, no longer – Montesquieu awaits."

A funny story is duly delivered.

And it really is very funny.

Everybody laughs, including Jocelyne, whom I invite to talk things over during break-time, if she feels like it.

"But until then, you're to think of nothing *except* Montesquieu."

Break time. Jocelyne tells me why she is so unhappy. Her parents aren't getting on. They argue from morning till night. They say terrible things to each other. Life at home is hell, the situation is heartbreaking. Here we go, I think to myself, another pair of long-distance runners who've taken twenty years to realize they're badly matched; divorce is on the cards. Jocelyne, who isn't a bad student, has taken a nosedive in all her subjects. And here I am, trying to patch up her blues. Perhaps, I say cautiously, divorce isn't such a . . . What I mean, Jocelyne, is that you might find two peaceful divorcees easier to deal with than a couple bent on destroying one another . . .

Etc.

Jocelyne bursts into tears again: "Actually, sir, they were going to get divorced, but they've just decided not to!"

Ah!

Right.

Right, right, right.

Well.

It's always more complicated than a novice psychologist might imagine.

". . ."

". . ."

"Do you know who Maisie Farange is?"

"No, who's that?"

"She's the daughter of Beale Farange and his wife. Two famous divorcees in their time. Maisie was very young when they separated, but nothing escaped her. You should make her acquaintance. In that novel. By the American. Henry James. *What Maisie Knew.*

A complex novel, incidentally, which Jocelyne read in the weeks that followed, inspired by the familiar terrain of conjugal battle. ("They're arguing just like the Faranges, sir!")

Oh yes, just because they bleed real blood doesn't mean that warring couples or hurting children are any less literary.

That said, when Montesquieu honours us with his presence in the classroom, we owe it to ourselves to be present for Montesquieu.

5

Presence in the classroom . . . It's not easy for boys and girls to come up with fifty-five minutes of concentration, for five or six successive lessons, as stipulated by the rigid timetable that school makes out of our days.

What a headache, that timetable! Dividing up classes, subjects, hours and students according to the number of classrooms, class sizes, optional subjects, the availability of science labs and the incompatible wishes of a male teacher in this subject or a female teacher in that subject . . . Admittedly, the timetabler's skin is saved by the computer entrusted with such parameters: "*Sorry about your Wednesdays, Mrs So-and-So, but that's what the computer came up with.*"

"Fifty-five minutes of French," I used to tell my students, "is a short hour with a beginning, a middle and an end; an entire life, in other words."

Come off it, they could have replied, a lifetime in literature, which gives on to a lifetime in maths, which gives on to an entire existence in history, which propels you for no good reason into yet another life, English this time, or German, or a chemical or a musical one . . . That's a lot of reincarnations in one day. And there's no logic to it. Your timetable is straight out of *Alice in Wonderland*: we're having tea with the March Hare, next thing we know we're playing croquet with the Queen of Hearts. A day spent inside Lewis Carroll's cocktail shaker, a miniature wonderland – talk about gymnastics! And as if that wasn't bad enough, this shambles is manicured like a French garden, from fifty-five-minute copse to fifty-five-minute copse, as it pretends to be orderly. Only a day in the life of a psychoanalyst, or a salami in a delicatessen, is sliced into similarly identical segments. And this goes on every week of the year. Arbitrary, with no surprises: the worst possible combination!

Stop grumbling, dear students, it would be tempting to say, and put yourselves in our shoes. Your comparison with a psychoanalyst isn't a bad one, as it happens. There they are, spending every day in their consulting room, seeing the world's unhappiness on parade; while here we are in our classrooms, seeing its ignorance on parade, in groups of thirty-five and at fixed times, our whole lives long, which – whether you can do the maths or not – is much longer than your all-too-brief youth, as you will see . . .

Never ask a student to put himself in his teacher's shoes; the temptation to laugh will be too great. Never invite him to compare his time with ours: our time isn't his time, we don't evolve at the same rate of speed. As for talking about ourselves or about him, absolutely not: off-limits. Let's stick to what we agreed: this hour of grammar will be a bubble in time. My job is to get my students to feel *grammatically alive* during these fifty-five minutes.

To achieve this, I must never lose sight of the fact that all lesson times are not alike: morning lessons are not the same as afternoon ones; the early hours of waking up, of digesting, those immediately before break and those immediately after, they're all different. The lesson that follows on from maths isn't the same as the one that comes after P.E. . . .

These differences have little effect on the attention spans of good students. They enjoy the blessed facility of being able to slip into a different skin whenever necessary, to shift from restless teenager to attentive student, from spurned sweetheart to focused scientist, from sporting hero to swot, from elsewhere to here, from past to present, from maths to literature . . . It's the speed with which they can inhabit the moment that distinguishes good students from challenged ones. The latter, as their teachers reproach them, and with good reason, are frequently elsewhere. They find it harder to free themselves from their previous lessons, as they lag behind in some memory or wish they were somewhere else. Their chair is an ejector seat, releasing them from the classroom the moment they sit down. Or else they fall asleep. If I want their full attention, I've got to help them settle into my lesson. How to do this? It's something you learn, on the job mainly, over many years. But one thing is certain: for my students to be present, *I* have to be present, for the whole class and for each individual in it, and I have to be present for my subject matter too, physically, intellectually and mentally, during the fifty-five minutes that my lesson will last.

6

Oh, the painful memory of lessons when I wasn't *there*. How I felt my students drifting away, floating off as I tried to gather my strength. That feeling of losing my class . . . I'm not here, they're not here, we've come unhitched. And yet, the hour passes. I play the part of the person giving a lesson, they play the part of listeners. Our collective expression is perfectly serious, blah-blah on one side, scribbling on the other, an inspector would be satisfied: as long as the shop *looks* open . . . But I'm not here, for heaven's sake, today I'm not here, I'm somewhere else. What I'm saying isn't grabbing their attention; they couldn't care less about what they're hearing. No questions, no answers. I'm hiding behind the well-oiled lesson. The energy I squander to make this ridiculous wisp of knowledge catch fire! I am a hundred leagues away from

Voltaire, from Rousseau, from Diderot, from this class, from this school, from this situation, and I'm wearing myself out trying to reduce the distance, but nothing doing; I'm as far away from my subject matter as I am from my class. I'm not a teacher, I'm a museum caretaker, giving them a compulsory guided tour-by-rote.

Those wasted lessons that brought me to my knees! I would leave the classroom exhausted and furious. The kind of fury my students risked paying for the entire day, since no-one is quicker to shout at you than a teacher unhappy with himself. Watch out, kids, hug the walls, your teacher has given himself a bad mark, the first "guilty" party to wander into the line of fire will do. And that's before marking your homework, come the evening, at home. A domain in which fatigue and a bad conscience are poor advisers. But no, no homework that evening, no television either, no going out, just bed. The teacher's key skill is sleep. The good teacher goes to bed early.

7

You can immediately tell if a teacher fully inhabits his classroom. Students sense it from the first minute of the school year, it's something we've all experienced: the teacher has just walked in, he is fully present, this is clear from the way he looks at his students, the way he greets them, the way he sits down, the way he takes ownership of his desk. He hasn't spread himself too thin, fearful of the students' reactions; his body language is open; from the word go, he's on the case; he is present, he can distinguish every single face, for him the class *exists.*

I recently experienced this kind of presence at Blanc-Mesnil, where I was invited by a young colleague who had immersed her students in one of my novels. What a morning I spent there! Bombarded with questions by readers who seemed to have a better grip than I did on the subject of my book, as well as the inner worlds of my characters, and who revelled in certain passages and enjoyed taking a swipe at my writer's tics . . . I'd been expecting to answer a series of sensibly prepared questions under the watchful eye of a teacher who'd be standing slightly to one side, mainly anxious to maintain discipline, as has frequently happened in my experience; but instead there I was, caught up in a whirlwind of literary controversy in which the students were asking me very few conventional questions. When their enthusiasm caused their voices to rise above a tolerable decibel level, their teacher questioned me herself, two octaves down, and then the entire class regrouped along this tonal register.

Later, over lunch in a café, I asked her how she managed to control so much lively energy.

To begin with, she was evasive: "The trick is never to talk louder than they do."

I wanted to know more about her expert handling of these students, their manifest happiness at being there, the relevance of their questions, the seriousness with which they listened, the way their enthusiasm was monitored, their self-restraint when they didn't agree with each other, the group's energy and cheerfulness, in short everything that contradicted the terrifying media stereotype of classrooms full of black and *beur* kids.

Having considered my questions, she replied: "When I'm with them or marking their homework, I'm not somewhere else."

She went on: "But, when I'm somewhere else, I'm not with them."

Her *somewhere else* was a string quartet that demanded her complete concentration as a cello player. What's more, she saw a natural parallel between a classroom and an orchestra.

"Each student plays his or her instrument, there's no point in arguing with that. The tricky part is knowing our musicians well enough to play in harmony. A good class isn't a military regiment marching to the same beat, but an orchestra working on the same symphony. And if you've inherited a triangle which can only go *ting-ting*, or a jew's harp which can only go *bloing-bloing*, what matters is that they do it at the right time, and to the best of their ability, that they become an excellent triangle, an irreproachable jew's harp, and that they're proud of what their contribution brings to the group. Since they're all inspired by a taste for harmony, even the triangle will end up knowing the music, perhaps not as brilliantly as the first violin, but to some level of familiarity at least."

Then she frowned: "The problems start when people try to make kids believe in a world where only first violins count . . ."

A pause.

"Or when my colleagues think they're von Karajan and don't take kindly to the idea of conducting the village band. They're all dreaming of the Berlin Philharmonic, which is understandable . . ."

As we said our goodbyes, I reiterated my admiration for what she was doing, prompting the reply: "Don't forget, you were there at ten o'clock. They were awake."

8

Morning registration. Hearing your name being spoken by the teacher is like the alarm going off a second time. At eight in the morning, your name vibrates like a tuning fork.

"I can't bring myself not to take the register, especially in the morning," another teacher tells me – a maths teacher, this time – "even if I'm in a hurry. I defy anyone to read out a list of names as if they were counting sheep. I look at my terrors as I call out their names, I welcome them, I name them one by one, and I listen to their responses.

After all, registration is the only moment in the day when a teacher addresses every student, if only to pronounce their surname. It's a nanosecond when the student knows that he or she *exists* for me, not anyone else. I try my best to gauge their mood from the sound of their 'Present'. If their voice falters, I know I'll have to reckon with that at some point."

The importance of taking the roll . . .

My students and I used to play a little game. I would call out their names, they would respond, and I would repeat each "Present" softly but in the same tone of voice, like a distant echo:

"Manuel?"

"Present!"

"*Present.* Laetitia?"

"Present!"

"*Present.* Victor?"

"Present!"

"*Present.* Carole?"

"Present!"

"*Present.* Rémi?"

I would imitate Manuel's restrained "*Present*", Laetitia's bright "*Present*", Victor's vigorous "*Present*", Carole's crystal-clear "*Present*" . . . I was their morning echo. Some of them tried to make their voices inscrutable, others enjoyed changing their intonation to take me by surprise, or answering “Yes” instead, or “Here”, or “That’s me”. Whatever their answer, I would repeat it very quietly, without betraying surprise. It was our complicit moment, the morning greeting for a team about to get down to work.

My friend Pierre, a teacher in Ivry, never takes the register.

“Well, two or three times at the beginning of the year, frequently enough for me to recognize their names and faces. But I like to move on to more serious matters as quickly as possible.”

His students wait in queues in the corridor at the door to his classroom. Everywhere else in the *collège*, they run around, yell, knock over tables and chairs, swarm the place, ratchet up the noise. But Pierre waits for the queues to form, then he opens the door; he watches the girls and boys walking in one by one, exchanges a relaxed hello with some of them; he then closes the door and goes purposefully over to his desk as the students stand behind their chairs. He invites them to sit down and begins: “Right, Karim, where were we?” His lesson is a conversation that picks up where it left off.

Because of the seriousness with which he approaches his work, the affectionate trust placed in him by his students and their loyalty once they’ve left school, my friend Pierre has always seemed like a reincarnation of Uncle Jules to me.

“You’re the Uncle Jules of Val-de-Marne!”

He laughs his tremendous laugh: “You’re right, my colleagues have got me pegged as a character out of the nineteenth century! They think I pay lip service to respect, that the kids queuing up, standing behind their chairs, all that business, is just nostalgia for the old days. It's true, a little politeness never hurts, but as it happens this is about something else. By giving my students a chance to settle down quietly, they're able to come to land properly in my lesson, to begin from a calm place. As for me, I get to scan their faces, note who's absent, see how cliques are forming or splitting up; in short, I get to take the class's temperature."

In the last lessons of the afternoon, when our students were dropping from exhaustion, Pierre and I used to engage in the same ritual without realizing it. We'd ask them to listen to the city (Ivry in his case, Paris in mine). Two minutes of stillness and silence in which the din outside confirmed the peace within. We spoke quietly during those lessons, often ending with a reading.

9

My generation has certainly spouted nonsense, writing off classroom rituals as a sign of blind submission: marking has been labelled as demeaning, dictation as reactionary, mental arithmetic as silly, memorization as infantile and so on . . .

The same goes for teaching as for everything else: as soon as we stop reflecting on individual cases (in this domain, every case is individual) in order to regulate our actions, we seek out the shadowy figure of good doctrine, the relevant authority, the guarantee of the decree, an ideological blank cheque, in order to protect ourselves. We pitch our tents on the ground of unshakeable certainty, however much daily experience may contradict it. Decades later, as the Ministry of Education tacks to avoid the looming iceberg of accumulated disasters, we might allow ourselves a timid adjustment of internal orientation; but it's the ship itself that is changing direction. And so we pass the headland of a new doctrine, sailing under a new admiral, in the name of our own free will, of course – dutiful students to the last.

10

So, dictation's reactionary? It's certainly ineffective if sloppily handled by a teacher interested only in deducting marks in order to arrive at a final score. And marking's demeaning? Most certainly, when it resembles that farce on television of a teacher handing exercise books back to students, each piece of homework presented like a verdict to a criminal, the teacher's face ablaze with fury and his running commentary condemning all those good-for-nothings to eternal ignorance and perpetual unemployment. My God, the hateful silence of that class. Contempt matched by contempt.

II

I've always thought of dictation as a head-on encounter with language. Language as sound, as story, as reasoning; language as it writes and constructs itself, meaning as clarified through meticulous correction. Because the only goal in correcting dictation is to access the text's precise meaning, the grammar's spirit, the words' richness. If the mark is meant to measure something, it is surely the distance covered by the interested parties on this journey towards understanding. Here, as in literary criticism, it's all about moving from the uniqueness of the text (what story am I going to be told?) to elucidating the sense (what does this mean exactly?), via a passionate interest in the way it functions (how does it work?).

However great my childhood terror when dictation loomed – and God knows my teachers administered it like wealthy raiders besieging a town's poorest quarter – I was always curious about that first reading. Every dictation begins with a mystery: what's about to be read to me? Some dictations from my childhood were so beautiful that they carried on dissolving inside me like a pear drop long after I'd received my ignominious mark. I turned that zero in spelling (or that -15, or -27!) into a refuge from which nobody could oust me. It was, I concluded, pointless wearing myself out with corrections when I already knew what my mark would be.

How many times, as a child, did I announce to my teachers what my students would, in turn, so often repeat to me:

"I always get zero in dictation!"

"Really, Nicolas? What makes you think so?"

"I've always got zero!"

"Me too, sir!"

"You too, Véronique?"

"And me, and me!"

"Then it must be an epidemic! Raise your hands, those of you who've always got zero in spelling."

This conversation took place at the beginning of the year, as we were getting to know each other, me and my class of thirteen-year-olds, for example. It inevitably led to the first in a long series of dictations:

"Okay, let's see. Take out a sheet of paper, and write 'Dictation' on it."

"Siiiiiir!"

"No arguing. 'Dictation'. Write: 'Nicolas claims that he will always get a zero in spelling' . . . 'Nicolas claims . . . '"

A dictation I made up as I went along, an immediate echo of their claim to being no-hopers:

> Nicolas claims that he will always get a zero in spelling for the simple reason that he has never obtained any other mark. Frédéric, Sami and Véronique share this view. This zero, which has hounded them since their first dictation, has caught up with them and swallowed them whole. From listening to them, you'd think that each of them lives inside a zero from which they will never escape. What they don't realize is that the key is in their pockets.

While I was making up the text, giving them each a small part to play in order to keep them interested, I was reviewing my grammatical accounts: past participle conjugated with *avoir*, pronoun as object; present tense singular preceded by plural pronoun complement and relative pronoun as subject, two more participles with *avoir* and a preceding pronoun as direct object; infinitive preceded by pronoun complement – and so on.

Once I'd finished dictating, we began our correcting:

"Right, Nicolas, read the first sentence."

"'Nicolas claims that he will always get a zero in spelling.'"

"Is that the first sentence? Are you sure it ends there?"

". . ."

"Read it carefully . . ."

"Ah! No, 'for the simple reason that he has never obtained any other mark'."

"Good. What is the first verb?"

"*Claims*?"

"Yes. What's the infinitive of 'claims'?"

"To claim."

"To which verb group does that belong?"

"Um . . ."

"Group Three. I'll explain in a minute. Tense?"

"Present."

"Subject?"

"Me. I mean, Nicolas."

"Person?"

"Third person singular."

"Third person of the verb 'to claim' in the present tense, yes. Pay attention to the ending. Your turn, Véronique. What is the last verb in the same sentence?"

"*Has*!"

"*Has*? From 'to have'? Are you sure? Read it again."

". . ."

". . ."

"Sorry, sir, it's *obtained.* The verb is 'to obtain'."

"Tense?"

This correction process takes us back to zero, which is where we said we were setting out from. With thirteen- and fourteen-year-olds? Yes! They can start again from zero. As can fifteen-year-olds. It's never too late to start again from zero, whatever the curriculum might say. I'm hardly going to rubber-stamp a lack of basic knowledge or pass a hot potato on to the next colleague. Let's start again from zero: each verb needs interrogating, each noun, each adjective, each link, step by step; what they're doing is reconstructing language with each dictation, word by word, verb group by verb group.

"*Reason,* common noun, feminine singular."

"What's the determiner?"

"The!"

"And what kind of a determiner is that?"

"An article!"

"What kind of article?"

"Definite!"

"Does *reason* have a qualifying adjective? If so, does it go before or after the noun? Elsewhere in the sentence or close by?"

"Before it: *simple.* There's no adjective after. Just *simple.*"

"Noun and adjective must agree, in case you've forgotten."

These dictations, daily fixtures for the first few weeks, took the form of short narratives kept as a class journal. They weren't prepared in advance. The final full stop opened on to a collective process of meticulous correcting. Then came the teacher's secret marking, which is to say mine, at home, before handing back their dictations the next day; the mark, that dreaded mark, it was all about seeing Nicolas's face when he escaped his zero for the first time. Nicolas's mug, or Véronique's, or Sami's, the day they smashed through the glass ceiling of spelling. They'd beaten fate! At last! Sweet moment of birth!

From dictation to dictation, the assimilation of grammatical reasoning prompted reflexes which sped up the marking process.

The dictionary champions did the rest. Theirs was the Olympic part of the exercise. A sort of sport. This involved, stopwatch in hand, finding the word we were after as quickly as possible, extrapolating it from the dictionary, correcting it, transplanting it to the class's collective exercise book as well as to individual notebooks, then moving on to the next word. I've always made it a priority to master the dictionary, and I've trained some prodigious athletes in this field, sportsmen and women from the age of twelve who could land on any given word in two seconds flat, three tops. Being able to connect alphabetical classification and the thickness of a dictionary was an area in which a good number of my students could wipe the floor with me. (And while we were at it, we extended our study of classification systems to bookshops and libraries by seeking out the authors, titles and publishers of the novels we were reading in class or talking about. The challenge was to be the first person to land on the title of his or her choice. Sometimes, the bookshop owner would even give the book to the winner.)

Our daily dictations continued until I handed the reins of the next one to a former "no-hoper": "Sami, please will you write tomorrow's dictation for us – it should be six lines long with two reflexive verbs, a participle with *avoir*, an infinitive from Group One, a demonstrative adjective, a possessive adjective, two or three difficult words that we've already encountered, and one or two details of your own choice."

Véronique, Sami, Nicolas and the rest composed their texts in turn, dictating them and leading the marking. We carried on until every student was able to fly with their own wings, could become, unaided, in the silence of their head, their own methodical marker.

The failures – there were some, of course – could, for the most part, be attributed to non-academic reasons such as undiagnosed dyslexia or deafness . . . The fifteen-year-old, for example, whose mistakes made no sense at all, substituting *a* for *i* or *e*, or *o* for *u*, and who, it turned out, couldn't hear high frequencies. It had never occurred to his mother that the boy might be partially deaf. When he came home from the market, having "forgotten" half the shopping list, when his reply to her question entirely missed the point, when he didn't appear to have heard what she'd said to him, lost as he was in his reading, or his jigsaw, or his model sailboat, she put his silences down to an endearing distractedness: “I always believed my son to be a great dreamer.” To imagine that he might be partially deaf was beyond her.

(An audiogram and a rigorous sight test should be mandatory for every child starting primary school. This would avoid the erroneous judgements of teachers, compensate for what families are unable to spot themselves and deliver students from unexplained mental agonies.)

Once every student had escaped from his or her zero, dictations became less frequent but longer: weekly literary dictations, dictations penned by Hugo, Valéry, Proust, Tournier, Kundera, some of them so magnificent that we learned them by heart, like this text from Cohen’s *Book of My Mother*:

> But why are men so spiteful? How astounded I am on this earth. Why are they so prompt to hate, so ill-tempered? Why do they love to take revenge and hasten to speak ill of you, they who are soon to die, poor things? The ghastly fate of human beings, who arrive on this earth, laugh, move, then suddenly move no more, does not make them good: is this not incredible? And why are they so quick to return rough answers, in a voice like the shriek of a cockatoo, if you speak to them gently, which makes them think you are unimportant – that is to say not dangerous? And so the tender-hearted must pretend to be cruel in order to be left in peace, or even – and this is tragic – to be

loved. Why not just retire to bed and sleep like a dog? Sleeping dogs have no fleas. Yes, let's sleep – sleep has the advantages of death without that one minor drawback. Let's go and settle down in the cosy coffin. Like a toothless man who takes out his dentures and puts them in a glass of water by his bed, I would like to take my brain out of its box, take out my poor devil of a heart which beats too fast, too conscientiously, take out my brain and my heart and bathe those two poor billionaires in refreshing solutions while I sleep like the little child I shall be no more. How few humans there are and all of a sudden the world is empty.

Then came the hour of glory, the day I turned over essays written by my seventeen-year-olds to my fourteen-year-olds, even to my twelve-year-olds, to have their spelling marked.

My students, with their gold stars for scoring zero, had metamorphosed into examiners. A flock of spelling sparrows swooped down on those essays.

"He's forgotten to make anything agree, sir!"

"She's written these sentences, and you don't know where they start or finish . . ."

"When I've corrected a mistake, what should I put in the margin?"

"Goodness me, whatever you like . . ."

Laughing protestations from the concerned parties as they read the comments of their pitiless markers:

"Honestly, look what he's written in the margin: 'Moron!' 'Idiot!' 'Clot!' And in red too!"

"I expect you forgot to make something agree . . ."

There followed, among the ranks of the older students, a self-correcting campaign which, in essence, borrowed the method applied by the younger students: checking verbs and nouns, making sure everything agreed – in short, committing themselves to a process of grammatical fine-tuning which had the added advantage of exposing the meandering nature of particular sentences, and therefore the imprecise nature of particular arguments. This in turn prompted the discovery, which was to be the subject of several lessons, that grammar is the first tool of organized thought, and that the dreaded parsing of sentences (of which they naturally had hideous memories) alters our thinking, which is in turn sharpened by the proper use of those famous subordinate clauses.

Even with the older students, we might still give ourselves a spot of dictation, as a way of assessing the role played by subordinate clauses in the development of a well-structured argument. One day, La Bruyère himself helped us out.

"Take out a clean sheet of paper and let's see how, by juxtaposing subordinate with main clauses, La Bruyère announces – in a single sentence! – the end of one world and the beginning of another. I'm going to read the text to you; I'll translate the old-fashioned words. Listen carefully. Then you're going to write. Take your time, I'll dictate slowly, and you'll go step by step, as if you were thinking it through for yourselves:"

> While great nobles are content to know nothing, not merely about matters of State and the interests of princes but about their own private affairs; while they remain ignorant of household administration and all that the head of a family should know, and pride themselves on this ignorance; while they let themselves be robbed and ruled by bailiffs, while they are satisfied with being gourmets or connoisseurs of wine, with frequenting *Thaïs* and *Phryne*, with talking about the first and second pack or about how many stages there are between Paris and Besonçon or Philisbourg, certain bourgeois have been learning all about the internal and external affairs of the kingdom, have studied the art of government, have become shrewd politicians, acquainted with the strength and weakness of the whole State, have sought promotion, have gained promotion, have risen high, grown powerful; and relieved the prince of part of his public responsibilities.

"And now the coup de grâce: 'Those nobles who once scorned them now revere them, happy if they become their sons-in-law.'

"Two main clauses, of which the second is elliptical – 'happy' (they are happy) – knitted together with two subordinate clauses, the relative 'who once scorned' and the final, murderous, conditional 'if they become their sons-in-law'."

12

Why not learn these texts off by heart? Why shouldn't we make literature our own? Because memorization has gone out of fashion? Should we let these pages fly away like dead leaves because they're past their season? Is it conceivable that such encounters might ever be forgotten? If these texts were sentient beings, if these exceptional pages had faces, vital statistics, a voice, a smile, a smell, wouldn't we spend the rest of our lives gnawing at our knuckles for having let them slip away? Why should we condemn ourselves to retaining the merest trace, which will fade in time to the memory of a trace . . . ? ("Yes, I vaguely remember having studied a text at *lycée*, who was it by again? La Bruyère? Montesquieu? Fénelon? Which century was it from, the seventeenth? the eighteenth? It described, in a single sentence, the seismic shift from one social order to another . . .") In the name of what do we practise this stupidity? Is it simply because the teachers of the past allegedly made us recite poetry that was often inane, and because, according to some old farts, the human memory was a muscle to train rather than a library to enrich? (Aha!) Those weekly poems of which we didn't understand a word, each poem erasing the one before it, as if the whole point was to drag us closer to oblivion. Did our teachers assign us these poems because they loved them, or because their own schoolmasters had drummed into them the idea that the texts belonged to the Pantheon of Dead Letters? In any event, I got stuck with yet more zeros. And yet more hours of detention. "It is clear, Pennacchioni, that we haven't learnt our recitation!" Oh yes I did, sir, I knew it last night when I was reciting it to my brother, it's just that last night it was poetry, but what you want from me this morning is a *recitation*, and I can't supply it on demand, sir, not just like that.

Not that I said any of this, of course; I was far too frightened. And I'm only revisiting that terrifying ordeal of reciting in front of the teacher as a way of understanding the contempt in which any demand on the memory is held these days. Is it in order to exorcise these ghosts that they've ruled against the finest pages from literature and philosophy being assimilated into students' brains? Texts banished *from* memory because a few idiots treated them as if they were purely exercises *in* memory? Then surely one form of stupidity has replaced another.

One might argue that an organized mind has no need to learn things by rote. Such a mind makes straight for the heart of the matter. It retains the sense of what it reads and, whatever the teacher says on the subject, has a real feeling for the beauty of any text. What's more, in the twinkling of an eye it can find whatever book you like in its library; it will land slap bang on the right lines in two minutes flat. I know, for example, where my La Bruyère awaits me, I can see it over there on its shelf, and my Conrad, and my Lermontov, and my Perros and my Chandler . . . my entire company is scattered alphabetically across that familiar landscape. Not to mention cyberspace, where I can, with the tip of my index finger, consult humanity's entire memory. Learning off by heart? At a time when memory is counted in gigabytes!

All of this may be true, but the essential truth lies elsewhere.

When I learn something off by heart, I'm not compensating for anything, I am adding to everything.

Language is the heart of the matter.

Dive into language, and everything is there.

Drain the cup and ask for more.

In making my students memorize so many texts (one per week, any given text to be recited on any day of the year), I was precipitating them, keen as they were, into the great flood of language, which rises up through the centuries to crash against our doors and surge through our houses. Of course they grumbled the first few times. They thought the water would be too cold, too deep, the waves too strong, their bodies too weak. And rightly so. They were scared stiff of diving in:

"I'll never make it!"

"I'm hopeless at remembering things." (Trying out this argument on *me*, an amnesiac from birth!)

"It's too long!"

"It's too difficult!" (To me, the duty cretin!)

"I mean, it's not like we talk in verse any more!"

(Aha!)

"Will it be marked, sir?" (And how!)

And that's ignoring the complaints about the implied insult to their maturity:

"Learn it off by heart? We're not babies!"

"I'm not a parrot!"

They were going for broke, which was fair enough. They said what they did because that's what was said to them. Sometimes by their parents – how evolved those parents were: "I beg your pardon, Mr Pennacchioni: you make them learn texts off by heart? But my son isn't a child any more!" Your son, dear madam, will never stop being a child when it comes to language, and you yourself a tiny baby, and me a ridiculous kid, and the same goes for all of us, small fry carried along by the great river gushing from the oral spring that is Literature. Your son will want to know what language he's swimming in as it carries him along, quenches his thirst and nourishes him, and he'll want to be a bearer of such beauty himself, and proudly so! Trust him, he'll love it, the taste of words in his mouth, the flares of thoughts going off inside his head, as he discovers his memory's prodigious capacity, its infinite suppleness: an echo chamber, an unprecedented space in which he can make the most magnificent sentences sing out, in which he can translate the brightest ideas into sounds; he'll be intoxicated by sub-linguistic swimming as he discovers the insatiable cave that is his memory; he'll love diving into language, going deep-sea fishing for texts, safe in the knowledge that he'll possess them for the rest of his life, that they'll become part of his identity, and that he'll be able to recite them spontaneously, to himself, just to taste the words. Bearer of a written tradition which, thanks to him, will have become an oral tradition again, he might even go so far as to say them aloud to someone else, to share them, to seduce or simply to show off – you never know. In so doing, he'll revive the connection with that time before writing when the survival of thought depended on voices alone. Talk to me about regression, and I'll talk to you about homecoming. Knowledge is, in the first instance, carnal. Our ears and eyes capture it, our mouths transmit it. Yes, it comes to us from books, but those books come out of us. A thought makes noise, and the taste for reading is born of the need to speak.

13

A final word. Don't worry, dear madam (I might add, when speaking to this mother who, across generations, never changes), all this beauty in your children's heads won't prevent them from chatting phonetically with their friends on the Internet, or sending text messages that make you screech like a white-tailed eagle: "My God, what spelling! How the youth of today express themselves! Where is school when we need it?" Rest assured, in making your children work, we won't do you out of your maternal angst.

14

So, one text per week, which we should be able to recite on any given day of the year, at the drop of a hat, myself included. Numbered, to make it more interesting. First week, Text Number 1. Twenty-third week, Text Number 23. With all the look of an idiotic system, these numbers-as-titles were part of the game, adding the delight of serendipity to the pride of knowledge.

"Amélie, recite Number 19 for us."

"Number 19? That's the one by Constant about shyness, the beginning of *Adolphe*."

"Spot on, we're all ears."

> His letters were affectionate, full of reasonable and considerate advice; but hardly were we together than he showed a constraint which I could not explain and which caused a painful reaction in me. I did not then know what timidity meant – that inner suffering which pursues you into old age, which forces the profoundest feelings back into the heart, chilling your words and deforming in your mouth whatever you try to say, allowing you to express yourself only in vague phrases or a somewhat bitter irony, as if you wanted to avenge yourself on your feelings for the pain you experienced at being unable to communicate them. I did not know that my father was timid, even with his son, and that often, having waited a long while for some sign of affection from me which his apparent coldness seemed to prohibit, he would leave me, his eyes moist with tears, and complain to others that I did not love him.

"Terrific. 18 out of 20. François, Number 8."

"8, that's Woody Allen! *The Lion and the Lamb*."

"Go on."

"'The lion and the lamb shall lie down together, but the lamb won't get much sleep.'"

"Perfect. 20 out of 20. Samuel, Number 12."

"12, that's *Émile* by Rousseau. His description of the state of man."

"Precisely."

"Hang on, sir. François gets 20 out of 20 with two lines by Woody, and I've got to recite half of *Émile*?"

"That's life's terrible lottery for you."

"Right."

> You trust in the present order of society, without thinking that this order is itself subject to inevitable revolutions, and it is impossible for you to foresee or prevent the one which may affect your children. The noble become commoners, the rich become poor, the monarch becomes subject. Are the blows of fate so rare that you can count on being exempted from them? We are approaching a state of crisis and the age of revolutions. Who can answer for what will become of you then? All that men have made, men may destroy. The only ineffaceable characters are those printed by nature; and nature does not make princes, rich men, or great lords. What, then, will this satrap whom you have raised only for greatness do in lowliness? What will this publican who knows how to live only with gold do in

> poverty? What will this gaudy imbecile, who does not know how to make use of himself and puts his being only in what is alien to himself, do when he is deprived of everything? Happy is the man who knows how to leave the station which leaves him and to remain a man in spite of fate! That vanquished king who, full of rage, wants to be buried under the debris of his throne may be praised as much as one pleases; I despise him. I see that he exists only by his crown, and that he is nothing at all if he is not a king. But he who loses it and does without it is then above it. From the rank of a king which a coward, a wicked man, or a madman can fill, he rises to the station of a man, which so few men know how to fill.

"Who could put it better?"

I didn't abandon my students to these texts. I dived in with them. Sometimes we would learn the most complex ones while analysing them together. I felt like a swimming instructor. The weakest found it hard to make any progress, heads sticking out of the water, clinging to the plank of my explanations, slowly, slowly; then they swam unaided, just a few clauses to begin with, until they could tackle a full paragraph without reading, off the tops of their heads. As soon as they understood what they were reading, they discovered their mnemonic skills, and often, before the end of the lesson, a good number of them would be able to recite an entire text, swimming the length of the pool without the instructor's help. They started to revel in their memories. They hadn't been expecting this at all. You'd have thought they'd discovered a new function, like growing flippers. Astonished at being able to remember so quickly, they'd repeat the text a second time, a third, without a hitch. Their inhibitions gone, they could understand what they'd memorized. It wasn't enough to recite a series of words, and it wasn't just in their memories that they were transforming themselves; it was in their ability to understand language, someone else's language, someone else's thoughts. They didn't recite *Émile*, they recreated Rousseau's thought processes. A proud feeling. It's not that you mistake yourself for Rousseau in moments like that, but still, Jean-Jacques' prescience is being expressed through *your* lips!

15

And sometimes they would play. They would train together, they would hold competitions or recite their texts in ways that went against the grain: fury, surprise, fear, stuttering, eloquence, passion; sometimes, one or other of them would imitate the president, a government minister, a singer, a television presenter . . . They played dangerous games as well, attempted perilous exercises in mental agility; they would set themselves acrobatic challenges like the one revealed to me by a class of sixteen-year-olds at an end-of-year dinner. (They had kept it secret, to astound their teacher.) Between the fruit and cheese courses, a girl called Caroline pointed at a boy called Sébastien: "Challenge: I want the first paragraph of Number 3, the second verse of Number 11, the fourth verse of Number 6 and the last sentence of Number 15."

Thus challenged, Sébastien assembled a mental patchwork which he recited almost without hesitation as a unique and quirky text. Then he set his own challenge: "Your turn. Give us *Le Pont Mirabeau.*"

And he specified the terms:

"Backwards."

"Easy."

And there, to my astounded ears, the Seine started to flow upstream under the Pont Mirabeau, last verse to first, until it disappeared under the Plateau de Langres. Satisfied, Caroline gave us the author's name: Erianillopa!

"What about you, sir? Can you do that?"

A schools inspector might not have appreciated the Seine flowing upstream, or a washing-machine jumbling an entire year's worth of texts, or my twelve-year-olds decorating our classroom with banners displaying their most spectacular spelling mistakes like so much booty. I might also have been reproached for allowing my oldest students to entrust their homework to the provocative marking of my youngest students. A case of flattering some in order to humiliate others? After all, this was no laughing matter. Don't panic, Mr Inspector, I'd have pleaded, it's important to know how to play with knowledge. Playfulness is the life-breath of effort, its other heartbeat; it doesn't detract from the seriousness of learning, it serves as its counterpoint. What's more, being playful with subject matter is all about training ourselves to master it. Never belittle the boxer who exercises with a skipping rope.

In mixing up their texts, my older students weren't showing a lack of respect for the grand dame of Literature, but celebrating their mastery of memory. They weren't disparaging knowledge, but innocently admiring each other's know-how. They were expressing pride through playfulness, not showing off. And they teased Rousseau too, they consoled Apollinaire, they entertained Corneille – who also liked a good joke, and who is probably finding eternity a tad long. Above all, they established an atmosphere of playful trust which reinforced their serious-mindedness. They had done with fear. This was their way of saying, of shouting: At last!

Sometimes I would join in.

We might subject stupidity to the severest scrutiny and study the effects of its cohabitation with the rarest intelligence. Filled with wonder but exhausted by our ascent of *Rameau's Nephew*, we might allow ourselves a Carambar break, for example. One chewy caramel bar per student (I had a budget set aside for this purpose). The person with the stupidest story on their sweet wrapper, the most insulting joke at the summit of understanding where we had pitched our tents, that person would win a second Carambar. Then we'd continue our ascent, light-footed and even more honoured to be paying a call on Diderot. We knew that if understanding a text involves a harsh and lonely conquest of the mind, the stupid joke establishes a relaxing complicity which only trusty friends can share. It's with our closest friends that we exchange the stupidest stories, as a way of paying implicit tribute to their refined minds. With everyone else, we play it smart, we show off our knowledge, we display it, we're out to impress.

16

So, who were my students? Some of them were the type of student I'd been at their age, the type you'll find in any institution where boys and girls who've been rejected by respectable *lycées* go to fail. Many were repeating a year and suffered from low self-esteem. Others simply felt sidelined by the system. To the point where such notions made them dizzy, some had lost all sense of how to make an effort, of how to carry on, of urgency, in short of work; so they let life slip through their fingers, devoting themselves (beginning in the 1980s) to rampant consumerism, "who cannot use their own hands, and who pride themselves on what is not really theirs" (Rousseau's reflection wasn't lost on them, albeit now in a material context).

Each case was different, of course. For example, the outstanding student at a provincial *lycée* whose school record had got him on board the steamship headed for the *grandes écoles*, only to discover that he was the last person aboard; so mortified was he that his hair started falling out in clumps: a nervous breakdown, at fifteen. Or the girl who slit her wrists ("Why did you do that?" "To see what'd happen!"). Or the girl who flirted with anorexia and bulimia, or the one who ran away, or the one who'd come over from Africa, traumatized by a bloody revolution. This one the son of an indefatigable concierge, that one the lethargic son of a diplomat who was never around. Some were destroyed by family troubles, others played on them shamelessly. Nothing surprised this Gothic widow, with her black eyes and purple lips; while this studded leather jacket with quiff and cowboy boots, who had escaped a technical *lycée* in Cachan to return to higher education, was amazed to discover that culture is available to everyone. They were boys and girls of their generation, the yobs of the 1970s, the punks and Goths of the 1980s, the new-agers of the 1990s; they caught fashions the way you catch a cold: fashions in clothes, music, food, games, electronics – they consumed the lot.

About half the students from my earliest time as a teacher, the

1970s, filled the so-called "remedial" classes of a *collège* in Soissons, and we were encouraged, with sardonic professional wit, to "try tough love" with these kids. Some already had police files. Others were the sons of Portuguese tenant farmers, of local shopkeepers or of the great landowners whose fields covered the immense plains to the east, plains which had grown fertile on all the young men slain by the European suicide of 1914–18. Our "yobs" shared the same premises as the "normal students", the same canteen, the same games, and this happy mix was to the credit of the head teacher. Since functional illiteracy isn't a new invention, I had to teach these "remedial" teenagers how to read and spell all over again; it was with them that we questioned the *there* they never got to. What they didn't realize was that it was simply about being in the now, being together and, in so doing, being oneself.

Their maths teacher and I taught them how to play chess, as well. And they didn't do badly at all. We made a giant chessboard mural, which they gave me when I left ("We'll make another one"), and which I still have. Their prowess at this supposedly difficult game (this was the era of the famous Spassky–Fischer championship match), the confidence they gained from beating classes from the neighbouring *lycée* ("We beat the Latin-heads, sir!"), translated into progress in maths and success in their B.E.P.C.s. At the end of the year we staged a multi-class production of *Ubu Roi. Ubu* directed by my friend Fanchon, who teaches in Marseille these days, and who is also a sort of Uncle Jules in her way, steely in her fight against all kinds of ignorance. With the local bishop in the audience, Father and Mother Ubu caused an uproar in their double bed. (The bed was a vertical one, so the royal couple could be admired even at the back of the gym where the play was being performed.)

So, from 1969 to 1995, not counting two years spent in an establishment where the pupils were hand-picked, most of my students were, as I myself had been, children and teenagers with varying degrees of learning difficulties. The worst-hit presented more or less the same symptoms as I had at their age: lack of self-confidence, completely unmotivated, inability to concentrate, lack of focus, a predilection for lying, involvement with gangs, alcohol sometimes, drugs too (so-called soft ones, but the kids were runny-eyed all the same, some mornings . . .).

They were *my* students. (This possessive pronoun doesn't signal ownership; it designates an interval of time, my teaching years, when my responsibility as a teacher was wholly engaged with those particular students.) Part of my job involved persuading those of *my* students who'd most given up on themselves that courtesy, rather than hitting out, predisposes one more effectively to reflection, that communal life gives you a sense of involvement, that the day and the hour for handing in a piece of homework are non-negotiable, that a rushed job of homework has to be redone, that this, that that, but that never, ever, would either my colleagues or I abandon them in midstream. For them to have a chance of getting *there,* we had to teach them afresh how to make an effort, give them a renewed taste for solitude and silence, above all a way to master their time and overcome boredom. Sometimes, I even advised them to try exercises in being bored, to improve their concentration. I asked them not to do *anything*: to avoid distractions, not to eat or drink (even conversation was off-limits), not to work either – in short, to do nothing, absolutely nothing.

"Boredom exercise this evening, twenty minutes of doing nothing before getting down to work."

"Not even listening to music?"

"Absolutely not!"

"Twenty minutes?"

"Twenty minutes. Watch in hand. 5:20 to 5:40. Go straight home, not a word to anyone, don't stop at any cafés along the way, don't be distracted by pinball machines, ignore your friends, go to your rooms, sit down on the ends of your beds, don't open your rucksacks, don't put on your M.P.3s, don't look at your Game Boys, just wait for twenty minutes, staring into space."

"Why?"

"Out of curiosity. Concentrate on time passing, don't miss a single minute, and tell me about it tomorrow."

"How can you be sure we did it?"

"I can't."

"And after twenty minutes?"

"Pounce on your homework like a starving person gobbling a meal."

17

If I had to characterize those lessons, I would say that my presumed dunces and I were fighting "illusory thinking", the sort of thinking which, as in fairy tales, makes us prisoners of a never-ending present. Deciding to have done with that zero in spelling, for example, is to escape illusory thinking. You break with your lot. You escape the vicious cycle. You awake. You venture into reality. You're in the present indicative. You begin to understand. The day will surely come when you'll wake up. A day, an hour! Nobody keeps biting the apple of nothingness forever. Life is no fairy tale; we aren't victims of some curse.

Perhaps this is what teaching is all about: dispensing with illusory thinking, ensuring that each lesson is a wake-up call.

Of course, I realize that this kind of declaration might seem exasperating to teachers lumbered with the toughest classes in the *banlieues.* And yes, these formulas may indeed appear trite from a considered sociological, political, economic, familial or cultural point of view . . . Still, illusory thinking plays a role which shouldn't be underestimated when it comes to the dunce's tenacity for staying buried at the bottom of his own existence. And it has always been that way, whatever his social background.

Illusory thinking . . . One day, I ask my seventeen-year-olds to write a description of the teacher who sets the questions for the *bac*. It's their written assignment: "Describe the teacher who sets the questions for the French *baccalauréat*." They aren't children any more, they have time to think, a week to devote to their essays; they can work out for themselves that a single teacher couldn't possibly prepare all the questions for the French *bac* across all the different regional education authorities, that this is probably done by a group, that the task is divided up, that a committee decides the contents according to the different syllabuses . . . Not a bit of it. Without exception, they painted portraits of a wise, bearded, lonely, omniscient old man who, from atop the Olympus of knowledge, decreed the questions for the *bac* like so many divine mysteries. I had devised this essay subject in order to see what image they had of Authority, and in this way to shed light on the nature of their inhibitions. Goal achieved. We immediately procured the annual records of the *bac*, made an inventory of all the essay questions from recent years, analysed them, studied their components, discovered that five or six themes cropped up repeatedly, and that these were invariably formulated in two or three ways. (Scarcely more complex, in summary, than the variations on a recipe for *canard à l'orange*: no duck, substitute chicken; no orange, use turnips. If you've got neither chicken nor duck, use a joint of beef and some carrots. The sauce stayed the same: you had to support your arguments with favourite quotations.) Fortified by this structured analysis, their next bit of homework was to set an exam question themselves.

"Will it be marked, sir?"

(How many times was I asked that question!)

"Of course. All labour merits a wage."

Fantastic! A single title marked as if it were a whole essay, what a godsend! They rubbed their hands in glee. They anticipated a reduced workload for the weekend. But I wasn't to worry, they would take the assignment seriously; they promised they'd think of a proper topic, a theme, a structure and all that, cross my heart and hope to die, sir! (At the end of the day, they found the idea of replacing the God-like examiner rather appealing.)

They didn't come off too badly. They had drafted their essay questions according to what they knew about their syllabus, as well as a few popular ideas of the time. I could have got them hired by the Ministry of Education.

One of the girls observed that not even the task of formulating the official questions was exempt from illusory thinking: "You will support your arguments with quotations taken from your favourite works."

What quotations, on the day of the *bac*, sir? Where's the candidate going to pluck them out of? Her head? Not everybody learns texts like we do! And what kind of favourite works? Will they want to hear about our favourite singers? About our favourite comic strips? A bit *illusory*, this formula, isn't it?"

"Not illusory, idealized."

The following week, all that remained was to tackle the questions they'd set themselves. I won't pretend that they approached excellence, but their hearts were in it; I harvested essays which owed little to illusory thinking, and they reaped marks which owed a good deal to understanding the imperatives of the *bac*.

18

"Will it be marked, sir?"

There was the question of marks, of course.

A crucial question, marking, if you want to deal with illusory thinking and, in so doing, fight against absurdity.

Whatever the subject, a teacher quickly discovers that for every question, the student being interrogated has three answers: the right one, the wrong one and the absurd one. During my own schooling, I abused the absurd a fair bit – "A fraction should always be reduced to its common denominator!" or, later on, "Sine *a* over sine *b* can be simplified as sine, remainder *a* over *b*!" One of the misapprehensions of my school days doubtless arose from my teachers marking my absurd answers as wrong answers. My answers didn't matter. Only one thing was certain: they would be marked.

Generally with a zero. I understood this early on. It was the best way of getting some peace, this zero. At least in the short term.

Therefore, the *sine qua non* to liberate the dunce from illusory thinking is the categorical refusal to mark his answer if it is absurd.

During the first grammar-correcting sessions with my "remedial" students who claimed they had a season ticket for scoring zero, there was no lack of absurd answers.

Our friend Sami, for example, aged thirteen.

"Sami, what is the first verb conjugated in this sentence?"

"*Vraiment*, sir, it's *vraiment.*"

"What makes you say that *vraiment* is a verb?"

"It ends in *-ent*!"

"So what's the infinitive?"

". . . ?"

"Come on! What is it? A Group One verb? *Vraimer*? *Je vraime, tu vraimes, il vraime*?"

". . ."

The absurd answer can be distinguished from the wrong answer in that it involves no attempt at reasoning whatsoever. It is often automatic, a mere reflex. The student isn't making a mistake; he is giving a nonsensical answer prompted by some kind of clue (here, the *-ent* ending). He is not answering the question he has been asked, but rather reacting to the fact that he has been asked at all. Is an answer expected? He gives one. Right, wrong, absurd; it doesn't matter. What's more, back at the beginning of his school career, he thought the rules of the game involved answering for answering's sake; he would jiggle up and down in his seat, his hand in the air, quivering with impatience: "Me, me, miss, I know! I know!" (Here I am! Here I am!), and then he would give any old answer. But, very quickly, we adapt. We know that the teacher expects the right answer. It may be that we haven't got that answer to hand. And we haven't got the wrong answer either. We've no idea what response we're meant to give. In fact, we're not even sure whether we've understood the question. Can I admit that to my teacher? Is silence an option? No. Better to give any old answer. With a little ingenuity, if possible. Was I wide of the mark, Sir? I'm sorry, honest I am. I tried, it didn't work, that's all, give me a zero and let's stay friends. The absurd answer comprises the diplomatic admission of ignorance which, in spite of everything, wants to maintain a connection. Of course, it can also express an act of blatant rebellion: he's getting on my nerves, this teacher, pushing me into a corner like this. Do *I* ask *him* questions? Well, *do* I?

In all these scenarios, marking the answer – by correcting a written test, for example – means agreeing to mark absolutely anything, and consequently committing an act of pedagogical absurdity oneself. Here, whether consciously or not, student and teacher demonstrate the same desire: the symbolic elimination of the other. In giving a nonsensical answer to the question my teacher has asked me, I cease to consider him as a teacher; he becomes an adult whom I flatter or annihilate through absurdity. In agreeing to consider my student's absurd answers as wrong, I stop seeing him as a student; he becomes irrelevant to the subject, someone I've relegated to the limbo of the perpetual zero. In doing this, I erase myself as a teacher: faced with this youngster who, in my opinion, is refusing to play out his role of being a student, I cease to function as a teacher. When I've got to write his school report, I can always fall back on his ignorance of the basics. Doesn't a student who mistakes the adverb *vraiment* for a Group One verb clearly lack basic knowledge? Absolutely. But wouldn't a teacher who pretended to interpret as wrong an answer that is manifestly absurd be better off devoting his life to gambling as well? At least then only his money, not his students' education, would be at risk.

The limbo of zero suits the dunce down to the ground (or so he thinks). It's a fortress from which nobody will attempt to oust him. He reinforces this fortress by collecting absurdities; he decorates it with explanations that vary according to his age, his mood, his background and his temperament – "I'm too stupid", "I'll never get there", "The teacher can't stand me", "I'm angry, man", "It's doing my head in" etc. – he shifts from the playing field of education to the waste-ground of personal relations, where everything becomes touchy and sensitive. Which is what the teacher does too, convinced that the student is *doing it on purpose.* What frequently prevents a teacher from recognizing an absurd answer as the devastating result of illusory thinking is the feeling that the student is deliberately making fun of him.

From that moment on, the schoolmaster imprisons himself in his own *there*: "I'll never get *there* with that kid."

No teacher is exempt from this kind of failure. My own scars still run deep. They are familiar ghosts, the hovering faces of those students I didn't know how to rescue from their *there*, who locked me inside mine: "This time, *there* really is nothing I can do."

19

"So, at last!"

"What do you mean, *at last*?"

I recognize this voice. It's been stalking me since I began this book. It's been lying in wait. On the lookout for weakness. It's the dunce I used to be. Ever vigilant. More inclined than the person I am today to cast a critical eye on my pedagogical professionalism. I've never been able to escape from it. We've grown old together.

"At last what?"

"At last we're getting down to your own *there.* Your *y* as a teacher. Your incompetence zone. Because, frankly, from reading this far, anyone would think you were an irreproachable teacher: *Excuse me while I rescue all the students with severe spelling difficulties that ever were; while I fill each and every one of you up with unforgettable literature; while I introduce order to the most confused of minds* . . . So, no failures then?"

". . ."

"A kid for whom your approach *just didn't take* – didn't that ever happen to you?"

You spiteful no-hoper, rising from the abyss to wake my ghosts. Thing is, it works. Three faces instantly appear. Three faces at the back of the class, final year at *lycée.* They've got the entire French syllabus to catch up on for their *bac*, but remain impervious to what I'm saying about Camus and *L'Étranger*, a set text for their oral exam. Present at every lesson but somewhere else altogether. Three punctual *strangers* whose interest I never once captured, and whose silence pushed me into that corner of teacherly authority, the well-oiled lesson. My three Meursaults. They became a kind of obsession. The rest of the class wasn't enough to distract me.

"Is that all?"

"..."

"Is that all? Were there only those three?"

No, there's Michel, barely seventeen, expelled from just about everywhere, taken into our school on my recommendation, who, in record time, wreaks institutional havoc on a monumental scale and ends up exploding to my face ("Fucking hell, I never asked you for anything!") before disappearing off into I don't know what kind of life.

"Do you want more examples? A gang of petty thieves who targeted department stores despite my lessons in ethics, will they do?"

"Let's just say that talking about it will make you feel better."

"Get lost; I know all about your no-hoper's delight in preaching to the whole world. If I'd listened to you, I would never have taught anybody; I'd have got up very early one morning and stepped off the cliff at La Gaude."

"But I'm still here," he sniggers, "by your side. The dunce walks sidewise and clings like the crab that he is: it's a question of etymology . . ."

End of conversation. Until the next one. He slips back inside me, leaving me feeling remorseful about those lessons I prepared in a rush, those piles of homework I handed back late despite my best intentions . . .

There it is – *there's* our moment as teachers . . . The confined space of our sudden exhaustions, where we tally the students we gave up on.

A dirty prison. We go round in circles, more concerned with finding someone to blame than finding solutions.

20

From listening to the buzzing of our pedagogical hive, you'd think that as soon as we feel discouraged, we're driven to find someone to blame. Indeed, the whole French education system appears to be structured in such a way that each of us can comfortably designate a guilty party:

"Didn't they learn how to behave at nursery?" asks a primary-school teacher faced with small children restless as balls in a pinball machine.

"What on earth did they spend their time doing in primary?" curses a *collège* teacher as he greets a group of eleven-year-olds he reckons to be illiterate.

"Can someone tell me what they learned up until now?" exclaims a *lycée* teacher, bemoaning sixteen-year-olds' lack of discernible vocabulary.

"Did they really make it through *lycée*?" wonders a university lecturer as he goes over his first batch of marking with a fine-tooth comb.

"Explain what the hell people do at university?" thunders an industrialist faced with young recruits.

"University produces exactly what your system requires," replies a recruit (no fool he), "ignorant slaves and blind customers! The *grandes écoles* format your foremen – sorry, your 'managers' – and your shareholders bank the dividends."

"Collapse of the family unit," laments the education minister.

"School isn't what it used to be," regrets the family.

To which can be added the internal tribulations of any self-respecting institution. The eternal quarrel between the Ancients and Moderns, for example:

"Shame on asinine pedagogues!" roar republican anti-demagogues.

"Down with state-sponsored elitism!" retaliate the pedagogues in the name of progress.

"The unions have got us in a stranglehold!" claim civil servants in the Ministry of Education.

"We're just going by the book!" retort the unions.

"You never got illiteracy statistics like that in my day!" deplores the old guard.

"In your day, people were only voted on to the board of school governors if they were *one of us*," mocks the tease. "The good old times, eh?"

"You're the spitting image of your mother!" thunders the incensed father.

"If you'd just been a bit stricter with him, we wouldn't be in this situation!" replies the outraged mother.

"How can I work in that kind of atmosphere?" complains the depressed teenager, bending the ear of the understanding teacher.

All the way down to the dunce, who, having systematically and ferociously seen his teacher off to hospital to be treated for a nervous breakdown, is the first to explain, without a trace of irony: "Mr So-and-So never showed much authority."

As if that's not enough, we can always point to the person inside ourselves who wears the cap of our incompetence.

"There's nothing I can do about it, I'm just like that," I wrote to my mother as the dunce I used to be, requesting that she exile Mr Hyde, who was preventing me from being Dr Jekyll, to the wilds of Africa.

21

Let us dream a refreshing dream. The teacher is young, direct, unscripted; she isn't crushed by the weight of inevitability; she is truly in the moment, and her classroom is full of students, parents, colleagues and employers from France and northern Spain who've been joined – chairs have been put out for them – by the ten most recent ministers of education.

"'*There's* nothing we can do about it'?" the young teacher asks.

No reply.

"Did I hear correctly? '*There*'s nothing we can do about it'?"

Silence.

The young teacher offers a piece of chalk to the most recent minister and says: "Write on the board: '*On n'y peut rien*'."

"I wasn't the one who said it," the minister protests. "It was the civil servants! It's the first thing they say to every new incumbent: 'Basically, minister, there's nothing we can do about it!' I can hardly be accused of having said such a thing, given all the reforms I've proposed. It really is no good blaming me if my genius for reform is being obstructed!"

"It doesn't matter who said it," the young teacher smiles back at him. "Write on the board: '*There*'s nothing we can do about it'."

On y peut rien.

"Add an *n'* before the *y*. It's part of the problem, that *n'*. No small part!"

On n'y peut rien.

"Perfect. Now, what do you think that *y* means?"

"I don't know."

"Well, my friends, we've got to find out what it stands for, this *y*, because otherwise we're done for."

IV

You're Doing It on Purpose

I didn't do it on purpose

I

The Vercors, last summer. We're having a drink, V. and I, on the terrace of La Bascule, watching lazily as Josette's herd returns from the fields. V. who, like me, has reached retirement age, asks what I'm writing at the moment. I tell him.

"Ah yes! The bad student! Now, that's something I know a thing or two about because – let me tell you – I was no Einstein at school."

A pause.

"So I left as soon as I could . . . *Easy now*!"

Josette is following the cows on her bicycle, flanked by two Border Collies trotting along in very white socks.

"I was a fool," V. continues, "but what can you do, at that age you won't listen to anything except your hormones."

Another pause.

"School has its uses, you know. If I'd stayed, I'd be a boss today – in charge of some multinational or other, I reckon – instead of slogging my guts out for a pittance. Evenin', Josette!"

". . ."

"In charge of pushing it over the edge, I mean. And once I'd seen it nose-dive into the abyss, I'd leave with a fat cheque and the chairman's congratulations."

The herd has moved past us.

"Instead of which . . ."

V. ponders. He seems tempted by autobiography, but gives up on the idea.

"Thing is, I didn't do it on purpose . . ."

He pauses.

"No, really. They always thought I was doing it on purpose, but I wasn't. I was like a puppy, chasing my own tail."

2

One of the most frequent accusations that families and teachers level at bad students is "You're doing it on purpose!" Whether this is an accusation ("Don't lie to me, you're doing it on purpose!"), or exasperation after the umpteenth excuse ("I can't believe this, you're doing it on purpose!"), or information destined for a third party but which the suspect has overheard by, for example, listening at his parents' door ("I'm telling you, the kid's doing it on purpose!"). How many times did I hear that accusation myself, and say it too, finger pointing at a student, or at my own daughter, when she was learning to read, if she was mumbling. Until the day I stopped and asked myself what I was saying.

You're doing it on purpose.

Whichever way you look at it, the star of the sentence is the adverbial phrase "on purpose". Scorning grammar, it links directly with the pronoun *you. You on purpose*! The verb "to do" is secondary, and the pronoun *it* entirely colourless. What's important here, what rings in the ears of the accused, is this *you on purpose*, reminding us of that pointed index finger.

You're the guilty one,

the *only* guilty one,

and *deliberately* guilty, to boot!

That's the message.

The adult's "You did it on purpose!" segues neatly into the "I didn't do it on purpose!" of the child who has done something stupid.

Expressed with vehemence but without illusions, "I didn't do it on purpose" invariably prompts one of the following responses:

"I should hope not!"

"Just as well!"

"That *would* be the last straw!"

This patter wasn't invented yesterday, and grown-ups the world over can come up with a witty retort, at least the first time.

In "I didn't do it on purpose", the adverbial phrase "on purpose" loses some of its impact; the verb "to do" doesn't win any, remaining a sort of auxiliary, and the pronoun *it* counts for nothing. What the culprit is trying to make us hear is the pronoun *I* linked to the negative *not.*

So, to the adult's "you on purpose", the child replies "I not".

No verb, no pronoun complement; there's just me, here, this *I*, blighted by this *not*, insisting that, in this matter, I don't belong to myself.

"But of course you did – *Tu l'as fait exprès!*"

"No, I didn't do it on purpose!"

"You on purpose!"

"I not!"

Two people talking *at* one another, needing to kick the ball into touch, to defer the outcome. We walk away from each other without answers or illusions, one side convinced that it hasn't been obeyed, the other that it hasn't been understood.

Grammar may have something to contribute here.

If we can agree, for example, to take an interest in the virtually invisible word left lying on the ground of the dispute, this *it*, which has, on the sly, been manipulating our conversation.

Come on, a little old-fashioned grammar exercise, just to see what happens, the way I used to do it with my "remedial" students.

"Who can tell me what type of word *le* is in '*Tu l'as fait exprès!*'"

"Me, me! It's an article, sir!"

"An article? Why is it an article?"

"Because of *le, la, les,* sir! Oh, and it's a *definite* article!"

Triumphant tone of voice. We've shown the teacher that we know something . . . *Un, une, des,* indefinite articles, *le, la, les,* definite articles, gotcha, it's in the bag.

"Oh really? A definite article? And where the devil is the noun that's defined by this article?"

". . ."

Everyone looks for it.

No noun.

Confusion.

It's not an article.

What is this *le*?

". . ."

". . ."

"It's a pronoun, sir!"

"Hurray! What kind of pronoun?"

"A personal pronoun!"

"What else?"

"A pronoun complement!"

Good. Very good. Spot on. Now, let's leave the classroom and analyse this pronoun complement among ourselves, as grown-ups. Approach with caution. Pronoun complements are dangerous words, anti-personnel mines buried beneath apparent meaning; they'll explode if you don't defuse them first. This *it*, for example . . . How many times did we stop to ask ourselves, when launching into the accusatory "You're doing it on purpose", what was being expressed by the pronoun complement *it* in each instance? Doing *what* on purpose? The most recent howler? No, the tone of voice in which we levelled this accusation (for tone also plays its part) makes it quite clear that the guilty party *always* does it on purpose, that he does it on purpose *each and every time*, that this latest howler only confirms his obstinacy.

So, doing *what* on purpose?

Not obeying me?

Not working?

Not concentrating?

Not understanding?

Not even trying to understand?

Putting up a fight?

Giving me a hard time?

Exasperating your teacher?

Driving your parents to despair?

Indulging your weaknesses?

Writing off your future by ruining your present?

Refusing to take anything seriously?That's what this is all about, isn't it: refusing to take things seriously? Being provocative?

All of the above, yes, if that's what you're after – all of the above.

Next comes the adverbial phrase. Why *on purpose*? To what end? What reason could he possibly have? He must have a goal, since he's doing it *on purpose.*

On purpose for what purpose?

The thrill of the moment? Just for the thrill of the moment? But the inevitable moment afterwards, the one he'll spend with me, will be an excruciating quarter of an hour, since I'll be giving him hell! Perhaps he just wants to muddle along, live a lazy life, indifferent to being ranted at? Perhaps he's some sort of hedonist? No, he knows that the joy of doing nothing comes at a price: scornful looks and disapproval, which in turn lead to self-loathing. So why, despite all of this, does he persist in doing it *on purpose*?

To earn the respect of other dunces? Because making an effort would be an act of betrayal? Is he deliberately playing at baddies vs goodies, youth vs age? Is this his way of blending in?

If you like. At any rate, here's today's pet theory: being a dunce is tribal; all bad students disappear into the rabble-ridden backwater of the *banlieue.* What's convenient about this explanation is that it relies on a sociological truth: the phenomenon of the *banlieue* exists, no doubt about it. But it ignores the individual kid who will, whether he's involved in gang culture or not, find himself alone at some point, alone faced with his failures, alone faced with his future, alone in the evening, faced with himself as he's going to bed. So let us consider him. Examine him carefully. Who'd put any value on his sense of wellbeing? Who could suspect him of doing *it on purpose*?

You're doing it on purpose . . .

The truth is that none of these explanations are entirely satisfactory. They can all be made to fit, but . . .

Now here's an idea:

Might it be that, ignoring all the rules of grammar, the pronoun *it* also refers to something outside the sentence? Ourselves, for example . . . The damage to the way we see ourselves. Our self-image, which requires a flattering mirror.

And might this *it* accuse the other person – here, the bad subject – of reflecting back on to me the image of a powerless and worried grown-up, the victim of a point-blank refusal that I can't understand? God knows the principles with which I wish to inculcate this child are sound! And the knowledge I make available to this student is completely legitimate!

My adult sense of isolation echoes that of the child.

You're doing it on purpose.

And when this applies to an entire classroom, when thirty students start doing it on purpose, the teacher in me feels like the victim of a cultural lynch mob. And if this *it* affects a whole generation – "It would never have happened in my day!" – if successive generations are doing it on purpose, then we are the last representatives of a dying species, survivors of the last era in which youth (ourselves, back then) was a condition we actually understood. We feel alone in our old age – still clear-headed, of course, vigilant, and how, terribly competent! – but only among ourselves, just as when we were young. We few remaining witnesses of civilized eras may continue to think straight, but we're excluded from what, despite our best endeavours, reality has become.

Excluded . . .

For the feeling of exclusion doesn't just affect people driven out beyond the umpteenth circle of the *périphérique*; it also threatens us, the powerful masses, the moment we stop understanding what is around us, as soon as the whiff of something alien infects the spirit of the times. How helpless we feel then. And how this prompts us to finger the guilty parties.

"You're doing it on purpose!"

Such a tiny pronoun, such a vast sense of isolation.

3

A brief digression about this sense of exclusion as experienced by the worried majority. When I was an adolescent, there were at least two of us *doing it on purpose*: Pablo Picasso and me. The genius and the dunce. The dunce did nothing and the genius did whatever he liked, but *on purpose*, both of them. It was the only thing we had in common.

Often, over Sunday lunch, the grown-ups would gossip about Picasso: Ghastly! Painting for snobs! Nonsense elevated to the status of serious art . . .

Despite all this commentary, Picasso spread like algae: drawings, paintings, etchings, ceramics, sculpture, set designs, even literature – anything went.

"Apparently, he simply dashes things off!"

Prolific algae from some monstrous ocean, intent on polluting the bays of peaceful art.

"He's an insult to my intelligence! I never let anyone make a fool of me."

Until one Sunday, when I took Picasso's side, asking the woman who'd just repeated this accusation for the umpteenth time if she *genuinely* believed that the artist had awakened that morning with the idea of knocking off a quick canvas for the sole purpose of making a fool of Mrs Geneviève Pellegrue.

The truth is that these respectable people were starting to feel excluded; they were becoming isolated. They accorded Picasso the terrifying power to overrun everything. The charlatan was creating a new universe meant for him alone, a menacing tomorrow in which a horde of Picassos would transform every Pellegrue in the world into one and the same dupe.

"Not me! He won't get me!"

Geneviève Pellegrue didn't realize that she was a stomach, that she'd digest Pablo Picasso just as she would everything else, slowly, yes, but inexorably, to the point that, forty years later, her grandchildren would drive around in one of the most hideous family cars ever conceived, a giant suppository which the new Pellegrues would name after the artist, and which would drop them off, one fine Sunday when the cultural itch got the better of them, at the doors of the Musée Picasso.

4

The aggressive oversimplifications perpetrated by vested interests . . . Oh yes, the upholders of a norm, whatever that might be: a cultural norm, a family norm, a business norm, a political norm, a religious norm, the norm of a clan, a club, a gang, an area, a standard of health, a standard of brawn or brain . . . How these guardians of the norm recoil the moment they get a whiff of something they don't understand, how they relish putting up a fight, you'd swear they were fending off some universal plot entirely on their own! This fear of being threatened by whatever breaks the mould . . . The aggressiveness of the powerful man playing at being the victim! Of the well-heeled when poverty camps on their doorsteps! Of the model couple confronted with the divorced woman, destroyer of relationships! Of natives sniffing out the diasporic! Of the believer singling out the heathen! Of the degree-holder sizing up the unfathomable cretin! Of the chauvinistic idiot overly proud of his birthplace! The same goes for the small-time gang leader, suspicious of the enemy on the pavement opposite . . . How dangerous those who've understood the codes become when faced with those who haven't.

Even children have to be on their guard.

5

I've never had a clearer sense of the pernicious fear experienced by someone who thinks they're being excluded, when confronted by others who really are, than one morning on my own.

I'm having a lie-in. Minne is somewhere in the south-west, visiting students at a technical *lycée* near Toulouse. A visiting writer. So, no amorous awakening under the influence of caffeine. I really should be working on my book, but no, I stay in bed, staring into space, just as I used to in front of the homework I wasn't doing ("Don't disturb the little one, he's working"). I switch on the radio. My favourite station. The right day and time for one of my favourite programmes. Once a week, it invites certified brains to speak in a tone of voice that's becoming increasingly rare these days, that of people with nothing to sell. Ideas are calmly exchanged about what they're writing, with well-judged references to what they've been reading. Just what I need on this lazy morning; they'll do my thinking for me. Don't tell anybody, but I'm about to consume other people's thoughts as lazily as if I was gorging on the first TV soap I'd switched on. Delicious. I salivate upon hearing the theme music, and, as soon as the contributors have been introduced, I allow myself to swoosh downwards in the sleigh of their sentences, to float gently upwards on their swirling arguments, and I feel good, in the land of knowledge, reassured by their affable voices, their limber phrasing, their considered opinions, their serious tone, their keen analyses, the irreproachable béchamel into which the presenter blends their different ideas, smoothing out potential disagreements, enthusiastically developing his own thoughts . . . I've always liked this programme, not least for its elegance; reality is polished to the point where I find it legible, if not reassuring.

It so happens that the chat, this particular morning, turns to the subject of "disaffected youth". At one point, my three voices are discussing a film. I prick up my ears. A film that seems to have traumatized the presenter. It's a film about the *banlieue.* No, it's a film about a play by Marivaux. No, it's a film about an educational project. Yes, there you go, it's a film about *lycée* students from the *banlieue* putting on a play by Marivaux, as directed by their French teacher. It's called *L'Esquive.* It's not a documentary. It's scripted like a documentary. It doesn't try to pass itself off as reality, it tries to provide the most faithful representation possible. I'm listening all the more attentively because I've seen the film in question. Not that I'd been keen: yet another film about school, once again set in the *banlieue* . . . Still, I went to see it, no doubt prompted by atavistic curiosity. (Shades of Uncle Jules: "Go and see *L'Esquive*, nephew, no ifs or buts!") And I enjoyed it: a teacher guides her students, via the medium of theatre, onto the highway of great literature. The class stages *The Game of Love and Chance* by Marivaux. We see the kids devoting energy and concentration to this exercise which doesn't detract from their own love stories, their problems at home and on the estate, their teenage rivalries, their involvement in small-time dealing, their difficulties with language, or even theatre's reputation as an activity for "*bouffons*". I left the cinema comforted by the conviction I derive from most of my visits to *lycées* in the *banlieue*: Uncle Jules lives! There are still Uncle Juleses and Aunt Julies who, despite the extraordinary challenge of such rescue operations, seek out their children wherever they may be, in order to raise them up to their true potential via the pathways of the French language, in this case that of the eighteenth century.

But this isn't how my radio presenter feels about it. He isn't the slightest bit reassured. No enthusiasm whatsoever. He left the cinema horrified by the young people's language outside the charmed circle of Marivaux. My God, their voices! The constant shouting, the violence, the impoverished vocabulary, that belching, the vulgarity of their insults! Ah, how he suffered during that film on behalf of the French language! How his French was injured! How he sensed it being threatened to its very core! Threatened, what am I saying? Condemned! Mercilessly condemned by this loathing of language! What would become of the French language? What would become of it, faced with these roaring hordes of dunces?

I didn't, unfortunately, record this purple passage, but that was essentially it; this wasn't a man talking about teenagers any more, no, it was the fear inside this man that was doing the talking. His interlocutors seemed rather surprised. The listener could guess at the gestures sketched to reassure the presenter, but in vain; fear won the day.

Alone in bed, my hair on end, I might have thought: You're mad to have let your wife go off to meet those savages; they'll eat her alive! Instead of which I wanted to give the presenter a reassuring hug. There, there, calm down; the under-dog has always spoken loudly, you know that, it's something he does, it's a geographical and historical given, the world over; and he speaks even more loudly because he's surrounded by more under-dogs, and they also speak loudly to make themselves heard, do you see? The poor man lives surrounded by paper-thin party walls. And while it's true he swears a lot, he means no harm by it, no, really, and the further south poverty heads, the more the poor man uses sexual swear words, or religious ones, or both at once. They come naturally to him. It's not as if he's met you so you could point out to him how bad it is. I mean, when I was a kid, the poor people in my village mean those who'd come up from the Italian south used to say "*Pute vierge*!", they never stopped saying "*Pute vierge*!", or "*Porca madonna*"; not that they had anything against either the Saturday-evening whore or the Sunday-morning Virgin, it was just what they said when they banged their fingers with a hammer. One whack of hammer on index finger and bam, a little oxymoron: *Pute vierge* . . . ! Did you know that the underclasses use oxymorons? Well, they do! So there you go, it's something we've got in common. We the pen, they the hammer, joined in oxymorons. Encouraging, don't you think?

That should assuage your fears about the flood of their sabir sweeping away the subtleties of our language. Oh, and there's something else I wanted to say: don't be afraid of their sabir. The sabir of today's under-dog is the slang of yesterday's under-dog, no more, no less. The under-dog has spoken in slang forever. You know why? To make the rich man think the poor man has got something to hide! He hasn't got anything to hide, of course, he's much too poor, nothing but a spot of small-time dealing here and there, trifles, but he's determined to make it look as if he's hiding an entire world, a universe that's forbidden to the rest of us, so huge that he needs an entire language to express it. But there is no world, and no language either. Just a small lexicon for those in the know, about staying warm, about camouflaging despair.

Slang isn't a language, it's merely vocabulary; the grammar of the disempowered is our grammar, reduced to its bare minimum, granted – subject, verb, complement – but ours, yours, don't worry, your very own French grammar, a grammar that belongs to all of us; the under-dogs need our grammar to understand each other. They've still got their vocabulary, of course, these young people from the umpteenth circle of the *banlieue*; a remarkably poor vocabulary in your opinion (considered from your lofty height, it would look like that). But, once again, don't worry, the under-dog's lexicon is so poor that most of these words are quickly carried off by the winds of history: they're twigs, just twigs, too little thought to weigh them down. Hardly any of them land in the dictionary. Take the back-slang of young people today – I researched a few words of *verlan*, a bit half-heartedly, I'll admit, gave them less than fifteen minutes, but all I could find in the dictionary were *meuf*, *keuf* and *teuf*. Not much, three common nouns for *woman*, *cop*, *party* – *femme* and *flic* and *fête* – spliced and flipped backwards, and that will disappear once the page of our era has been turned; dictionaries offer the merest glimpse of eternity . . .

A final word, so you feel completely reassured: go to the post office, pay a visit to your local council, ride on public transport, go into a museum or a benefits office, and you'll see, you'll see, it'll be the mother, the father, the brother or the older sister of these young people with their deplorable language who'll welcome you, sitting behind the counter. Or do as I did, fall ill, wake up in hospital, and you'll recognize the accent of the young male nurse pushing you on a trolley towards the operating theatre: "No stress, bro, they'll fix you up good as new, innit!"

6

To cap it all, one of the very first questions I'm asked by students in the *banlieue* classrooms to which their teachers have invited me is about the coarseness of my language. Why are there so many swear words in my novels? (Oh yes, my friend, your terrifying teenagers share your preoccupation: why is there so much linguistic violence?) Agreed, they ask me this question in order to please their teacher, a little, to try and make me feel embarrassed, sometimes, but also because for them a word only becomes truly rude when it's written down. We might call someone a "wanker" to their face, or claim not to give a "flying f**k" during break, or threaten to "screw your mum" like there's no tomorrow, but finding *wanker* and *screw* and *fuck* in black on white, in a book, when their place is on loo walls, that's something else entirely . . . !

It's at this point in our exchange that, more often than not, these students and I strike up a conversation about the French language: beginning with the slang in my novels, then moving on to slang as a language of substitution, of dissimulation, of always being in the know; about how it gets used, violently of course, but also affectionately (slang words, more than any others, are tone-sensitive – there's nothing like them when it comes to shifting from insult to caress); about its ancient origins in a country that has been working towards linguistic unity for centuries; about how wide-ranging it is: the slang of outlaws, the slang of urban areas, of guilds, of classes, of communities; about its progressive assimilation into the dominant language and about the role literature has played, from Villon down to the present day, in this slow process of digestion (hence the presence of swear words in my novels) . . . One thing leads to another, and so we find ourselves talking about the history of words:

"Words have a history, they don't fall from our mouths like freshly laid eggs! Words evolve, their lives are as unpredictable as our own. Some end up meaning the opposite of what they meant in the first instance: the adjective *énervé*, for example, used to designate a frog whose nerves had been removed, a poor little creature reduced to a puddle, certainly not Mouloud, here, today, whose neighbour is *getting on his nerves* and who is, at the end of the day, becoming *énervé*, as in vexed, man! Words can even drift as far as slang. Take the poor cow, the *vache*, so peaceful in its pasture, but which, over time, has come to signify so many unpopular figures: in the twelfth century, the prostitute; in the late nineteenth century, the policeman; today, all the baddies who commit *vacheries*! The modest cow, who has engendered, goodness knows why, the mother of superlatives: *vachement*.

It was in the course of one of these conversations that a teacher asked her students: "Can somebody give me an example of a 'normal' word that has turned into one of your slang words?"

". . ."

"Come on! A word you say a hundred times a day when you're having a laugh at someone's expense?"

". . ."

". . ."

"*Bouffon*, miss? Is *bouffon* one?"

"Yes, *bouffon*, for example."

". . ."

Bouffon: I heard it for the first time in the early '90s, walking into my classroom one morning when two little cockerels, spurs at the ready, were warming up for a fight: "He called me a *bouffon*, sir!"

Bouffon, which goes back to thirteenth-century Italy, where it referred to court jesters, erupted in front of me that morning as a synonym for *loser*. Fifteen years on, for the students in the class I was visiting, as for those in *L'Esquive* and, more generally, for young people of the same background and generation, the insult refers to anybody who doesn't share their codes – in other words, what young people of my mother's generation called the *bourgeoisie*, even though this was precisely what they themselves were ("He's *so* middle-class . . .").

Bourgeois . . . Now there's a word that's been through the mill. From aristocratic disdain to workers' anger by way of young Romantic rage, anathema to Surrealists, universally condemned by Marxist-Leninists, scourge of artists of every kind, it has been so larded by history with pejorative connotations that not one child of the bourgeoisie would openly describe himself as middle-class without a profound sense of shame.

Middle-class fear of the poor man, and the poor man's contempt of the middle classes . . . Yesterday, the leather jacket of my teenage years was all it took to frighten the middle classes, then along came the *yobs* to alarm the nobs; today, it's the youths from the estates who terrify the *bouffons.* And yet, just as yesterday's *bourgeois* had little chance of encountering a leather jacket, so today's *bouffon* runs little risk of crossing paths with a teenager doomed to faraway concrete stairwells.

How many kids from the estates had our radio presenter, so frightened by the teenagers in *L'Esquive*, dealt with personally? Could he count them on the fingers of one hand? No matter, it's enough to hear them talking in a film, to listen to thirty seconds of their music on the radio, to see cars burning in the *banlieue*, for him to be seized by a kind of generalized terror, to dismiss them as the army of dunces destined to bring our civilization to its knees.

V

Maximilien, or the Ideal Culprit

Teachers, they do our heads in, sir!

I

Belleville, a winter's evening, darkness has fallen over Rue Julien-Lacroix; I'm heading home, pipe in mouth, bag of groceries, mind adrift, when a guy leaning against a wall stops me, his arm drops like a parking barrier. My heart skips a beat.

"Givvus a light."

Just like that, no more respect for the forty years that separate us. He's tall, eighteen or twenty, black, well-built, trading on his menacing calm, confident of his strength and getting his way: he demands a light, he's given one, end of story.

I put down my bag of groceries, take out my lighter, hold the flame towards his cigarette. He lowers his head, hollows his cheeks as he inhales and, for the first time, looks at me over the red, glowing tip. His attitude changes. His eyes pop, his arm drops again, he takes the cigarette out of his mouth and stammers: "Oh! Sorry . . ."

Hesitation.

"You're not . . . ? You write . . . You're a writer, aren't you?"

Here we go, I might think to myself with a ripple of pleasure, a reader. But an old instinct whispers something else: a student, that's what he is. His French teacher's probably assigned him a *Malaussène* for his oral exam; in a second he'll be asking me to give him a hand.

"Yes, I write books, why?"

And I'm not wrong.

"Because our teacher, she's making us read *The Fairy, The Fairy* . . ."

So he knows there's the word fairy in the title.

"It's about Belleville and old ladies, and . . ."

"*The Fairy Gunmother*, yes. And?"

And he's a kid again, twiddling his hair before asking the decisive question:

"We've got to hand in an essay about the book. D'you think you could help me out a bit, give me some tips?"

I pick up my bag of groceries.

"Did you see how you asked me for a light?"

Embarrassment.

"You wanted to frighten me."

Protestation: "No, on my mum's life."

"Don't endanger your mother. You wanted to frighten me." (I'm careful not to add that he nearly succeeded.) "And I'm not the first. How many people did you speak to like that today?"

". . ."

"Except that you recognized me, and now you want me to help you. But what are people supposed to do when you haven't been set homework about them, and your arm's blocking their way? They're frightened and you're satisfied, is that it?"

"No, sir, come on . . ."

"But respect is something you know all about, isn't it? It's a word you use a hundred times a day. You've just shown me disrespect and you want me to help you?"

". . ."

"What's your name?"

"Max." He quickly adds his full name: "Maximilien!"

"Well, Maximilien, you've missed your chance. That's where I live, over there, Rue Lesage, those windows up there. If you'd asked politely for a light, that's where we'd be, and I'd be helping you with your homework. But now it's not going to happen."

Last try: "Come on, sir . . ."

"Next time, Maximilien, when you talk to people respectfully, but not this evening; this evening, you've made me angry."

2

I often think back on my encounter with Maximilien. An odd experience for both of us. Within a matter of seconds, I found myself trembling in front of a hoodie and saving face before a student. He got a buzz out of intimidating a *bouffon*, then blanched in the presence of a Victor Hugo type (in Belleville, some of the kids I'd watched grow up would jokingly call me Mr Hugo). Maximilien and I experienced two versions of each other: the hoodlum to fear or the student to help, the *bouffon* to intimidate or the writer to importune. Fortunately, the glow of a lighter muddled the two versions. For a second, we were both hoodie *and* student, *bouffon and* novelist; reality became more complex. If we'd got no further, if Maximilien hadn't recognized me, I'd have returned home ashamed of my near panic in the face of so-called "scum", and he'd have got a buzz from spooking an old "*bouffon*". He could have bragged about it to his friends, and I could have complained into a microphone. Life would have stayed simple: the hoodie from the estate humiliating the intelligent citizen, an interpretation conforming to the delusions of our times. Fortunately, the flame from a lighter revealed a more complex reality: an encounter between a teenager with plenty to learn and a grown-up with lots to teach him. Including this: If you want to become emperor, Maximilien, if only of yourself, then you need to drop the scare tactics; don't add a single grain of truth to the image of the terrifying dunce that is being calmly constructed behind your back by hacks with microphones pretending to quake in their boots.

"Yeah, right . . ."

As I read what I've just written, a little snigger wells up inside me.

"Right, right, right . . ."

There's no mistaking that sarcastic tone; it's him of course, the dunce I used to be.

"Just look at you with your fine words! Didn't Maximilien come in for a nice moral lecture?"

And, to hammer it home: "An overdose of smugness perhaps?"

". . ."

"What I'm saying is, you didn't help that student . . ."

". . ."

"Because he wasn't polite?"

". . ."

"And you're proud of yourself?"

". . ."

"What happened to your principles? Those high and mighty principles you set out earlier on. Remember: 'Fear of reading is cured . . .' Those sorts of declarations. Where've they disappeared to?"

". . ."

"Basically, you messed up, that evening, with Maximilien. Maybe you were too angry, or too afraid; even you can feel frightened, especially when you're tired. You know you should have taken that boy by the arm, brought him home with you, helped him with his essay, had a chat, even given him hell, but *after* you'd completed the homework assignment. Responding to his request, that was what mattered, since, as it happens, there *was* a request. Badly expressed? Agreed. Self-interested? All requests are self-interested, you know that. It's your job to transform calculated interest into an interest in the text. But by deserting Maximilien, by leaving him standing on the pavement while you headed home, you kept the wall between you intact. Reinforced it, even. There's a fable by La Fontaine about that. Would you like me to recite it? You play the lead role!"

The Child and the Schoolmaster

A little boy was mucking about on the banks of the Seine
When he lost his balance and landed in the stream.
A willow branch hung down, on which he managed to obtain
A purchase and this, after God, assured his safety, it would seem.
Now as he grasped the tree's abundant greenery
Who should pass by to grace this charming scenery
But a teacher to whom the unhappy creature
Yelled, "Save me! I'm about to die!"
The master stopped and turned upon hearing this cry,
And decided that a stern lecture is what would meet the case,
Even though one might have regarded this as neither the time nor place.
"Now just look at the little ape! See what occurs when he has to play the fool!
He expects a teacher to watch over him even out of school?
Pity," he said, "the parents of this useless lad –

His poor old Mum and Dad –
Just think what they have to endure day in day out:
It must be hell, I'm sure, the task of bringing up this little lout!"
Having delivered himself of these sentiments, the master,
Considering that the boy risked being drowned,
Reached over, plucked him up and set him on solid ground –
Though some of us might feel he should have been there faster.
My story blames more folk than may at first appear: I'd say
All bletherers, all captious or censorious persons, all pedants may well
Observe themselves in this tale I've had to tell.
Each of the three makes an abundant class:
The Creator has bidden them increase
And multiply and fill the earth en masse.
Any excuse suffices that they might exercise their tongues and never cease.
So now, just listen to me, mate:
Give me a hand first, and after that, go on and perorate.

3

Maximilien is the face of the contemporary dunce. When you hear about school today, you're hearing about him. Twelve million four hundred thousand French students pass through our schools every year, including about a million teenagers from immigrant backgrounds. Let's suppose that two hundred thousand might be in educational freefall. How many of those two hundred thousand have tipped over into verbal or physical violence (insulting teachers, whose lives become a living hell, behaving in a threatening manner, lashing out, damaging school premises . . .)? Let's say a quarter. Which makes fifty thousand. It follows that out of a population of twelve million four hundred thousand students, it only takes 0.4 per cent to keep the image of Maximilien alive: that ghastly nightmare of the dunce set on wrecking civilization, who monopolizes our channels of information as soon as we start talking about school, who turns even the most considered of imaginations febrile.

Let's say I'm wrong in my calculations, and that we should double or triple my 0.4 per cent; the figure remains derisory, and the fear engendered entirely shameful for the grown-ups that we are.

A teenager from a high-rise just outside the *périphérique*, whether Black, *Beur* or relegated Gaul, a fan of designer brands and mobile phones, a free radical who moves in groups, hooded to the chin, a tagger of walls and trains, a fan of mashed-up music with vengeful lyrics, his bite allegedly as bad as his noisy bark, suspected of being a rioter, dealer, arsonist or religious extremist in the making, Maximilien is the contemporary face of the working-class suburbs of yesteryear. Just as, in the old days, the bourgeois liked to mix with the riff-raff on the Rue de Lappe, or go dancing in the open-air dives on the banks of the

Marne where low-life gangsters hung out, so today's *bouffon* likes to rub shoulders with Maximilien, but only as an image, an image he stews up from the fancy ingredients of cinema, books, advertising and the news. Maximilien is both the image that inspires fear and the face that sells, the hero of increasingly violent films and the wearer of the most popular clothing brands. If Maximilien himself is confined to the margins (town planners, housing costs and the police all see to that), his image is beamed into the affluent heart of the city, where the *bouffon* is appalled to see his own children dressing like Maximilien, adopting Maximilien's slang, even, horror of horrors, tuning their voices to mimic the sounds Maximilien emits. From there, it's just one step to roaring the death of the French language and the imminent demise of civilization, a step taken quickly and with delicious anticipation, because we know, deep down, that Maximilien is the one who's being sacrificed.

4

Close up, Maximilien is the opposite of a shining example of "youth". Our times have made being young compulsory: you've got to be young, you've got to think young, to consume young, you've got to grow old youthfully, fashion's all about youth, football's all about youth, radio stations are about youth, magazines are about youth, advertising's young, television's crammed with young people, the Internet's young, the last remaining baby boomers have managed to stay youthful, even our politicians look younger now. Long live youth! Glory to youth! We've got to be young!

As long as we're not Maximilien.

5

"Teachers, they do our heads in, sir!"

"You're mistaken. Your head's been done in already. Teachers are trying to give it back to you."

This conversation took place at a technical *lycée* on the outskirts of Lyon. To reach the school in question, I had to cross a no-man's-land consisting of all sorts of warehouses, where I didn't meet a living soul. A ten-minute trudge between high, blind walls and concrete silos with composite roofs was the pleasant morning walk that life offered students from the nearby high-rises.

What did we talk about, that day? About reading, of course, and writing too, about how stories come into novelists' heads, about what "style" means (when it's not a *look*); about the difference between a real person and the notion of a character, and consequently of *bovaryisme* – mistaking a fictional character for a real person – as well as the danger of indulging this habit for too long after you've finished reading the novel (or seen the film); about reality and imagination, about the one being passed off as the other in reality tv shows. All topics that fire up students from every walk of life as soon as they give them some serious thought . . . And we talked, more generally, about their relationship with culture. It goes without saying that this was the first time they'd seen a writer; none of them had been to the theatre before, in fact very few had even got as far as Lyon itself. When I asked them why, their answer wasn't slow in coming: "So, like, we go there and all those *bouffons* call us scum, innit!"

In short, all was as it should be: the city was frightened of them, and they were scared of being judged by the city . . . As with many young people of their generation, both boys and girls, most of them were so tall you'd think they'd grown up between the walls of warehouses, in search of sunlight. Some were fashionably dressed – *their* fashion, they thought, although their clothes were uniformly global – and they all overdid the rap accent that affects even the trendiest *bouffons* from urban centres, where these students didn't dare show their faces.

We started talking about their studies.

It was at this point that the duty Maximilien intervened. (Yes, I've decided to give all the dunces in this book, whether from *banlieue* or chic neighbourhood, this handsome, superlative name.)

"Teachers, they do our head in!"

He was visibly the class dunce. (That adverb "visibly" speaks volumes, for the fact is you can quickly spot the dunce in any class. In all the schools I'm invited to, whether plush establishments, technical *lycées* or *collèges* servicing estates, Maximiliens are easily identified by their awkward concentration or by that exaggeratedly kind look their teachers give them when they speak in class, by the smiles waiting to happen on the faces of their peers, by something about their voices that doesn't sound quite right, their tone apologetic or vehement but slightly shaky too. And when they don't say anything – often Maximilien doesn't say anything – I recognize them by their worried or hostile silence, so different from the attentive silence of the student who's taking everything in. The dunce forever lurches between apologizing for being alive and wanting to exist in spite of everything, to find his place, to assert it even, through violence, his anti-depressant.)

"What d'you mean, teachers do your head in?"

"They do our heads in, you get me – with all their pointless stuff."

"Can you give me an example of this pointless stuff?"

"It's like, *everything*. I mean . . . subjects! They're not real life!"

"What's your name?"

"Maximilien."

"Well, you're mistaken, Maximilien, teachers aren't doing your heads in, they're trying to give them back to you. Because your heads are already done in."

"What d'you mean, my head's already done in?"

"What are you wearing on your feet?"

"On my feet? I've got my N.'s, sir!" (Here, the name of the brand.)

"Your what?"

"My N.'s, I've got my N.'s!"

"And what are your N.'s?"

"What d'you mean? They're my N.'s!"

"As an object, I mean, what kind of object are they?"

"They're my N.'s!"

And, since I wasn't in the business of humiliating Maximilien, I opened the question out to the others: "What is Maximilien wearing on his feet?"

Exchanged glances, an embarrassed silence; we'd just spent an enjoyable hour together, we'd discussed, reflected, joked, laughed a lot, they were ready to help me out here, but they had to agree, Maximilien was right: "They're his N.'s, sir."

"Yes, alright, I can see, they're N.'s, but as an object, what kind of object are they?"

Silence.

Then, suddenly, a girl: "Oh, I get it, what kind of object? They're trainers!"

"That's right. And might you have a more general noun than 'trainers' to describe this kind of object?"

"Er . . . shoes?"

"There we go, they're trainers, shoes, pumps, kicks, sneakers, call them what you like, but not N.'s! N. is the brand, and a brand is not an object!"

A question from their teacher: "If the object is for walking in, what's the point of the brand?"

A flare goes up at the back: "For flaunting it, miss!"

The teacher: "For showing off, yes."

A fresh question from the teacher, who points to the pullover being worn by another boy.

"What about you, Samir, what are you wearing?"

"It's my L., Miss!"

At this juncture, I mimed acute agony, as if Samir had just poisoned me and I was dying in front of them, when someone else laughed and called out: "No, no, it's a *pull*, his L.! It's a pullover! It's okay, sir, stay with us."

Resurrection: "Yes, it's his *pull*, and even if the word pullover is English in origin, that's still better than a brand name! My mother would have said: his jumper, my grandmother: his woolly; it's an old word, "woolly", but still better than a brand name, because it's the brands, Maximilien, that are doing your head in, not the teachers. They're doing your head in, your brands: They're my N.'s, it's my L., it's my T., it's my X., they're my Y.'s! They're doing your head in, they're doing you out of money, they're doing you out of words, and they're doing you out of your body too, like a uniform, they're making living advertisements out of you, like department-store dummies."

Here, I tell them about how there were sandwich-board men in my childhood, how I can still remember one or two of them standing on the pavement opposite where I lived, an old man strapped between two placards that peddled a brand of mustard.

"Brands do the same thing to us," I observe.

Maximilien, who's no fool: "Except with us, right, we don't get paid!"

A girl pipes up: "Nah, like in town, yeah, they get hold of the big shots by the school gates, the ones who like to strut, and they give them garms for free, so they can flaunt it in class, innit. Then all their crew go crazy for it, and that sells the brand."

Maximilien: "Nice one!"

Their teacher: "You think so? I think your brands are very expensive, but they're *worth* a lot less than you."

There follows an in-depth discussion about the notions of cost and value, not venal values, the other sort, those famous values, the ones these kids are supposed to have lost all sense of . . .

We parted ways with a little verbal demonstration: "Free-the-words! – Free-the-words!" until all their familiar objects – shoes, rucksacks, pens, pullovers, anoraks, M.P.3s, baseball caps, mobiles, glasses – had been stripped of their brands to reclaim their names.

6

The next day, back in Paris, as I was heading down the hills of the 20th arrondissement towards my office, I decided to put a street value on the students I saw along my way, using a simple calculation: 100 Euros for trainers, 110 for jeans, 120 for a jacket, 80 for a rucksack, 180 for an M.P.3 (a tour of your ear at 90 devastating decibels), 90 for a multi-function mobile phone, and that's without taking into account the contents of their pencil cases, which I'll do you for a knock-down price, 50 Euros, and the whole lot mounted on brand-new rollerblades, 150 Euros a pair. Total: 880 Euros (5,764 francs) per student, which is to say 576,400 of my childhood francs. Over the days that followed I compared my estimates with the prices in shop windows. All my calculations ended up at around half a million. Each of those kids was worth half a million of my childhood francs! And that's an average estimate per child of average background with parents of average income in Paris today. The price of a newly kitted-out Parisian student, let's say, at the end the Christmas holidays, in a society that sees its young people as customers, above all, as a market, as a field of targets.

Child customers, then, with or without means, from affluent city centre and *banlieue* alike, sucked in by the same ambition to consume, by the same universal hoover of desires, rich and poor, big and little, boys and girls, siphoned willy-nilly by that whirling entreaty: Consume! Meaning: Switch products; it's got to be new, better than new, the very latest model. Flaunt that brand! If their brands were medals, the kids in our streets would clink like caricature generals. Highbrow programmes go to great lengths to explain that this is simply an aspect of young people's identities.

September, first day back at school, and on the radio a high priestess of marketing, sounding for all the world like a responsible grandmother, declares that schools should allow advertising as an alternative information provider – after all, isn't information the bread and butter of teaching? Q.E.D. My ears prick up. What are you telling us here, Mrs Marketing, in your resonant, wise grandmother's voice? Advertising under the same heading as science, art, the humanities? Granny, you can't be serious! But she is, the minx. Diabolically so.

Oh, and she isn't holding forth on her own behalf, but on behalf of *life as it really is.* Life according to Granny Marketing looms suddenly in my imagination: a gigantic shopping centre without walls, limits or barriers, with no other objective than to consume. The ideal school (according to Granny): a rich seam of increasingly greedy consumers. The teachers' mission: to prepare students to push their shopping trolleys up and down the never-ending aisles of retail life. Let's stop protecting them from consumerism, Granny hammers out her words; let them emerge "informed" from the ghetto of education!

The ghetto of education: that's how Granny refers to school. Education reduced to information. Did you hear that, Uncle Jules? Those kids you saved from familial idiocy, whom you plucked out of the maquis of prejudice and ignorance, all that was merely in order to bang them up in the ghetto of education, fancy that! And you, my cellist in Blanc-Mesnil, did you know that in awakening your students to the joys of literature rather than advertising, you were merely acting as a blind warder in the ghetto of education? Teachers, when will you listen to Granny? When will you get it into your skulls that the universe isn't there to be understood but to be consumed? It isn't Pascal's *Pensées*, or the *Discourse on Method*, or the *Critique of Pure Reason*, or Spinoza, or Sartre that you should be putting in your students' hands, dear philosophers, but the *Big Catalogue for Making the Best of Life As It Really Is.* Come on, Grannykins, I spotted you behind your verbal disguise, you're the wicked wolf from the storybooks. Wrapped up snug in your bewitching logic, you lie in wait at the school gates, mouth wide open, ready to gobble up those Little Red Hoodies, with Maximilien out in front, of course, less able to defend himself than the others. How delicious to gobble up that head filled with cravings while the poor teachers try to wrench it away from you, poorly armed as they are, with their two hours of this, their three hours of that, against your formidable advertising artillery. Mouth wide open at the school gates, Grannykins, and it works. It's been going from strength to strength since the mid-1970s. The ones you gobble up today are the children of those you gobbled up yesterday. Yesterday, my students, today the progeny of my students. Whole families busy mistaking their every whim for vital needs in the appalling mix of your persuasive digestion. Reduced, all of them, big and little, to the same childish state of perpetual craving. More! More! shouts the consumed race of consumers from the bottom of your stomach, children and parents all mixed up. More! More! And it goes without saying that Maximilien is shouting the loudest.

7

I left my young students from their *banlieue* of Lyon with a bitter taste in my mouth. Those kids were abandoned in an urban desert. Their *lycée* was invisible, lost in a labyrinth of warehouses. Their estate wasn't much cheerier. Not a café in sight, not a cinema, not a living thing, nothing to rest your eyes on bar gigantic hoardings peddling objects beyond their reach . . .

So how can these young people be reproached for their perpetual posturing, for this image of themselves created for the public mirror of the group? It's all too easy to poke fun at their need to be seen when they're hidden from the world in this way, and have so little to see themselves. But beyond the temptation to exist *as images*, what are we offering these young people who'll inherit unemployment, whom the whim of history has, for the most part, forbidden a past and deprived of a geography? Where else can they find any repose – in the sense of having a rest, letting yourself go a little, *putting yourself back together again* – if not in the game of appearances? For this, according to Granny Marketing, is what identity is all about: clothing young people in appearances, satisfying the perpetual desire to be photogenic . . . Good God, what a rival for teachers, this hawker of readymade images!

In the train on my way back, I think about how, in going home, it's not just my house that I'm returning to: I'm reconnecting with my history, I'll be curling up at the centre of my geography. When I walk through my own front door, I enter a space where I was already myself long before I was born: the least notable object, the most insignificant book in my library, attests to my age-old identity . . . It's not very difficult, there, to escape the temptation of the image.

These are all things Minne and I talk about that evening.

"Don't underestimate those kids," she says, "and don't forget their energy! Or how clear-headed they become, once their teenage crises are behind them. A lot of them come through."

She cites friends who've come through. Including, and above all, Ali, who could easily have gone to the bad and who, today, is diving back into the heart of the problem to rescue those teenagers most at risk. Since they're victims of imagery, it's through learning how to manipulate images that Ali has decided to retrieve them. He provides the kids with cameras and shows them how to film their teenage life as it really is.

"These kids are in freefall at school," Ali explains to me, "a lot of them raised by single mums; some have already been in trouble with the police, they don't want to have anything to do with adults, they find themselves in Pupil Referral Units, something like your 'remedial' classes from the 1970s, I suppose. I take the class ringleaders who are fifteen or sixteen, I separate them temporarily from the group, because it's the group that's killing them, always, it stops them from being themselves; I stick a camera in their hands and have them interview one of their mates, someone they choose themselves. They carry out the interview on their own, away from prying eyes; then we view the film together, as a group.

"It never fails: the interviewee plays up in front of the lens, and the person filming enters into the game. They're trying to be clever, they big up their accents, they pull out all the stops with their slang while shouting as loudly as they can, like I did when I was a kid; they go over the top, as if they're addressing the whole group, as if the only possible audience is the group, and their friends have a good laugh during the screening. I show the film a second time, a third, a fourth time. The laughter becomes more intermittent, less confident. Both interviewers and interviewee can sense something strange happening, which they can't identify. On the fifth or sixth screening, genuine unease sets in on all sides. On the seventh or eighth (no, really, I've been known to screen the same film nine times!), they've understood, without me having to explain, that what we're seeing on the screen is them showing off, being ridiculous. It's all fake – their daily act, their mimicry, their escape mechanisms – and where's the interest in that? Zero; it's not real. Once they've understood this, I end the screenings and send them back with the camera to re-shoot the interview.

"This time we get something more serious that bears some relation to their actual lives: they introduce themselves, they tell us their surnames, their first names, they talk about their families, the situation at school; there are silences, they struggle to find the right words, we can see them thinking, interviewee and interviewer alike, and, little by little, we see their own *experience of being a teenager*; they stop being youths who are out to frighten people, they become boys and girls of their own ages again, fifteen, sixteen; their personal experience cuts through their appearance, it imposes itself; their clothes and baseball caps become accessories again, they don't gesticulate so much; instinctively, the kid doing the filming tightens the frame, zooms in, it's the face that counts now, as if the interviewer was *listening to the other person's face*; and what we can see on this face is the effort to understand, as if they're looking at each other for the first time, as they really are: they're getting to grips with complexity."

8

Minne tells me that in the younger classes she visits, she plays a game which the children love: the village game. It's simple enough; it involves chatting with them, discovering their individual characteristics, their talents and desires, the hobbies of this child and that one, then transforming the class into a village where everybody has their place, one they all agree is absolutely key: the baker, the postman, the primary-school teacher, the garage owner, the grocer, the doctor, the chemist, the farmer, the plumber, the musician. Each person has their place, including those for whom Minne invents key imaginary professions – dream collector or cloud painter . . .

"And what do you do with the class troublemaker? The 0.4 per cent, the outlaw; what you do turn him into?"

She smiles: "The cop, of course."

9

Alas, we can't eliminate the real outlaw, the killer, the one who can never be transformed into a cop, not even in jest. He is extremely rare, but he does exist. At school, just as everywhere else. In twenty-five years, during which I taught roughly two thousand five hundred students, I must have encountered him once or twice. I've seen him in court too, this teenager with his precocious anger, his icy expression; you knew he was bound to end up as a news story, because he couldn't control his urges, didn't pull his punches, stoked up his rage, planned his revenge, enjoyed hurting others, terrorized witnesses and remained impervious to remorse once his crime had been committed. There was that eighteen-year-old boy, for example, who smashed young K.'s spine with an axe, simply because K. came from another neighbourhood. Or the fifteen-year-old who stabbed his French teacher. Or that girl who'd been privately educated, a mediocre student by day but by night the seductress of forty-year-olds she delivered to two sidekicks of her own age and background, who proceeded to torture them to death in order to rob them. After her cross-examination, she asked the dumbfounded police officers if she could go home.

Those were not ordinary teenagers. Crime remains the mystery of our species, even when we use all the socio-psychological factors imaginable to explain it away. It's hardly surprising that physical violence increases with poverty, confinement, unemployment and the temptations of a society geared to gratification, but for a fifteen-year-old boy to plan to stab his teacher – and to do it – remains a singular pathological act. To make of this, amid a blaze of newspaper headlines and television reports, a symbol of a specific group of young people in a particular place (the *banlieue* classroom) is tantamount to dismissing that group as a den of assassins and that school as a breeding ground for criminals.

When it comes to murder, it's not unhelpful to remember that once you've ruled out armed attacks, public brawls, heinous crimes and the settling of scores between rival gangs, about 80 per cent of murders take place within families. More than anywhere else, men kill each other at home, under their own roofs, in the secret ferment where they live, at the heart of their own misery.

To pass school off as a place that encourages crime is, in itself, a senseless crime against school.

10

If you believe the zeitgeist, violence entered our schools only yesterday, solely via the *banlieue* and the immigration channels. Before that, it didn't exist. This is a dogma, not up for discussion. Yet I still remember those poor people we tortured with our unruliness in the '60s, that exasperated teacher hurling his desk at our class, for example, or that supervisor taken away in handcuffs for beating up a student who'd driven him to the brink of madness, or, at the beginning of the '80s, those supposedly sensible girls who'd forced their teacher to resort to sleep therapy (I was his replacement) because he'd dared to make them keep company with *La Princesse de Clèves*, which, those young ladies declared, was "dead boring" . . .

In the '70s – this time of the nineteenth century – Alphonse Daudet was already expressing his pain as a tortured school supervisor:

> So I was put in possession of a class of intermediates.
>
> In it I found about fifty mischievous boys, chubby-cheeked young mountaineers from twelve to fourteen years old. They were sons of farmers who had made money and had sent their boys to school to get them made into little bourgeois, upon payment of a hundred and twenty francs a quarter.
>
> Rough, rude, and arrogant, speaking among themselves only a coarse dialect of the Cévennes which I could not understand, they had, almost all of them, the kind of ugliness peculiar to boys just growing up; big hands covered with chilblains, voices like braying donkeys, brutal expressions, and

above all the rest, a special school flavour. They hated me at once, before they knew me. For them, I was the enemy, the under-master, and from the first day that I took my seat in their classroom, there was war between us, war relentless, continual, unremitting.

Ah, cruel boys, how they made me suffer!

I should like to speak of it without bitterness, for those melancholy times are now so far distant; and yet, I cannot, for, if you will believe it, as I write these lines, I feel my hand tremble feverishly with emotion. I seem to be back there again . . .

It is so terrible to live in the midst of ill-will, to be always afraid, always on the lookout, always angry and in arms; it is so terrible to punish, for one can be unjust against his will, – so terrible to doubt, to be watching everywhere the pitfalls, not to be able to eat or sleep in peace, and to be always thinking, even in a quiet moment: "O God! What are they going to do now?"

Come off it, Daudet, you're exaggerating; take it from us, you'll have to wait a good century for violence to enter our schools! And not via the Cévennes, Daudet, but via the *banlieue*, the one and only *banlieue*!

II

In the past, the dunce was depicted standing in a corner, a dunce's cap jammed down on his head. This picture didn't stigmatize any particular social group; it showed a child, any child, stood in the corner for not learning his lessons, for not doing his homework or for behaving in an unruly fashion towards Mr Daudet, the eponymous *Little What's-His-Name.*

Today, and for the first time in our history, an entire group of children and teenagers is being systematically stigmatized, on a daily basis, as token dunces. We don't put them in the corner, we don't stick dunces' caps on their heads, the word "dunce" itself has fallen out of use, and racism has supposedly been named and shamed – yet we film them endlessly; we single them out for all of France to see; we write articles about the wrongdoings of a few of them, presenting all of them as some kind of incurable cancer in the body of our education system. Inflicting educational apartheid on them isn't enough, no, we have to think of them as some kind of national disease: they represent *all* young people from *all* the *banlieues.* Dunces, the whole lot of them, in the public imagination, dunces and dangerous: school means *them,* since we only talk about them when we talk about school.

Since we only talk about school in order to talk about them.

12

True, there's no comparison between some of the abuses committed today (extortion rackets, teachers beaten up, *lycées* burned down, rape) and the educational unruliness of yesteryear, which was limited to relatively controlled violence within school walls. Rare as they may be, the symbolic weight of these misdeeds is terrible and their propagation almost instantaneous through images on television, on the Web and via mobile phones, all of which significantly increase the risk of copying.

A visit, a while back, to a *lycée* near Digne; I'm due to meet several classes there.

Spend the night at a hotel.

Insomnia.

Television.

Reportage.

Paris, the Champ-de-Mars, small groups of young people on the fringes of a student demonstration, attacking victims at random. One of the victims falls, a boy the same age as his attackers. They beat him. He gets up, they chase him, he falls again, they beat him again. The scenes multiply. Always the same scenario: the victim is chosen at random, on impulse, by someone in a group, which, transformed into a pack, sets on him fiercely. The pack runs after anything that runs away, each member egged on by another member, generating a dynamic of which he is himself the motor. They run at the speed of missiles. Later in the programme, a father will say of his son that he was forced into it, which is true, at least in the kinetic sense: the person being led turns leader. Does our friend Maximilien belong to one of these groups? The idea crosses my mind. But the attacks are so gratuitous that Maximilien might equally find himself among the victims; no time for introductions, this kind of violence is blind, immediate, extreme. (There's a warning against anyone under the age of twelve watching the programme. It must initially have been broadcast before the watershed, and I can imagine crowds of kids, enticed by the ban, gluing their faces to the screen.) The commentary comes from a police officer and a psychologist. The psychologist talks about the virtualization of a world without work, drowning in violent images; the police officer invokes the trauma of victims and the responsibility of perpetrators. Both are right, of course, but they give the impression of occupying two irreconcilable camps, as indicated by the psychologist's open-necked shirt and the officer's carefully knotted tie.

Next we follow four young people apprehended for killing a barman. They beat him to death, for fun. A girl filmed the scene on her mobile. She even took a kick at the victim's head, as if it were a football. The police superintendent who arrested them confirms a total loss of any sense of reality and, consequently, of any moral conscience. These four had spent the night indulging in their idea of fun: beating people up and filming it. We see them, thanks to C.C.T.V., going from one attack to another, perfectly laid back about it, like those A.W.O.L. friends in *Clockwork Orange.* Filming such acts on mobiles is a new trend, the commentator tells us. A young woman, a teacher, was one of the victims, in her own classroom (pictures). They show her, thrown to the ground by a student, beaten up, being filmed. Today, anyone can easily download a scene like this. You can even watch it to the music of your choice. Jaded commentary from some teenagers as they screen the film of the battered teacher.

I change channels.

An astounding number of violent films are available. It's a calm night, Mr Average is snoring peacefully, but at the foot of his bed, in the dark silence of his television, the images watch over him. People are killing each other in every way, to every rhythm, over and over again. Modern humanity stages the continuous murder of modern humanity. One channel has been spared, and on it, far from any trace of humankind, in the photogenic peace of nature, animals are tearing each other to pieces. To music, again.

I switch back to the first channel. A cheerful lad whose job involves downloading all the scenes of extreme violence filmed by the world (lynchings, suicides, accidents, ambushes, bombs, murders etc.) is justifying his dirty work with the classic refrain about the need to inform. If he didn't do it, other people would, he insists; he isn't violent himself, he's just the messenger. An ordinary bastard who keeps the engine ticking over, just like Granny Marketing; he might even be her son, and a decent family man too, for all I know . . .

I switch off.

No way of getting to sleep. I'm tempted to opt for apocalyptic pessimism. There's systematic impoverishment on the one hand, terror and general barbarity on the other. Both camps are completely cut off from reality: financial abstractions among the affluent, video massacres among the outlaws; the unemployed man transformed into the notion of an unemployed man by majority shareholders, the victim into the image of a victim by hoodlums. In each instance, a human mind, body and spirit are made to disappear. The media orchestrate this bloody opera in which commentaries lead us to think that *all* kids from the *banlieues* have the potential to race into the streets to exterminate the next person who, in their minds, is nothing more than the image of the next person. Where does education come into it? Where's school? Culture? Reading? Reason? Language? What's the point of me turning up tomorrow if the students I'm going to meet are likely to have spent the night in the guts of this television?

Sleep.

Wake up.

Shower.

Head under cold water, a nice moment.

Good God, the energy it takes to *return to reality* after seeing all that! Hell's bells, the image we're given of young people based on a few crackpots! I reject it. Let's be clear: I'm not denying the reality behind such reportage, I'm not underestimating the dangers of delinquency. The contemporary forms of urban violence horrify me, much as they do everyone else: I fear the pack's killer instinct; I'm not unaware of the pain of living in certain areas outside the *périphérique*; I can sense the dangers of segregated communities; I know, for example, about the difficulties of being born a girl in those neighbourhoods and of becoming a woman there; I can gauge the extreme risks facing children born into one or two generations of unemployment, what prey they are for dealers of every stripe. I know this, and I don't minimize the difficulties for teachers confronted by those students who've been most cut loose by this appalling social mess. But I refuse to conflate these images of extreme violence with all teenagers from *all* "at risk" areas, and, above all, above all, I loathe the fear of the underclass which this kind of propaganda stirs up with each new electoral cycle. Shame on those who turn the most neglected of young people into a mirage of national terror. They are the dregs of a society without honour which has lost everything, right down to its sense of paternal responsibility.

13

It turns out there's a celebration at the *lycée* that morning; it's the school festival. An entire *lycée* transformed for two or three days into an exhibition space for everything the students have created in the course of their extra-curricular activities – paintings, music, theatre, even architecture (they've built the display stands themselves) – led by a headmistress and a team of teachers who know every girl and boy by their first names. In the hall, a small student orchestra. The violin accompanies me along the corridors. Three or four classes are waiting for me in a huge room. We spend two hours playing freely at the game of questions and answers. Their liveliness, their laughter, their earnestness, their insights and, more than anything else, their vital energy, their staggering energy, rescue me from my television nightmare.

Return journey.

Station platform.

A message from Ali on my mobile: "Hi there! Don't forget our date tomorrow: my students are expecting you. They've finished editing their films. You've got to see how inspired these kids are!"

VI

What It Means to Love

In this world, you must be a bit too kind

in order to be kind enough

I

As soon as those desperate mothers hang up, I start dialling to find somewhere for their offspring to go. I do the rounds of colleagues – old friends, specialists in no-hopers – now it's my turn to play the role of tearful mum. On the other end of the line, they're having fun at my expense:

"Ah! You again! You usually pop up around this time of year."

"How many absences did you say? Thirty-seven! He skipped school thirty-seven times, and you want us to take him? Will you be delivering him in handcuffs?"

Didier, Philippe, Stella, Fanchon, Pierre, Françoise, Isabelle, Ali and the rest . . . Every single one of them has saved their fair share. Nicole H.'s *lycée* alone is open to all write-offs passing through . . .

I've even pleaded with them halfway through the school year.

"*Come on*, Philippe . . ."

"Why was he expelled? For fighting! On *and* off school premises? With security guards at a shopping mall! And it's not the first time? That's some Christmas present you're giving us! Send him over, I'll see what we can do."

Then there's Miss G., headmistress of a *collège*. She's busy supervising a written test. Under her scrutiny two classes slog it out. Silence. Concentration. Biros chewed or twizzled at high speed between thumb and index finger (how do they do that? I never could). Green rough paper for some, yellow for others . . . The calm of the study period. You could hear a pin drop. I've always enjoyed the silence of the siesta, the calm of the study period. As a child, the two were linked in my mind. I had a taste for unearned rest. I'm an expert in the art of pretending to write while preparing a blank answer paper. But it's hard to play that game when you're being supervised by Miss G.

She sees me coming out of the corner of her eye. She doesn't bat an eyelash. She knows I never disturb her without good reason, and that when I do so, it's rarely as the bearer of good tidings. I walk silently over to her desk and whisper my sales pitch in her ear: "Nearly sixteen, has been kept back a year, lost any work habit about ten years ago, expelled for countless reasons, arrested in the *métro* last month for dealing hash, mum on the run, irresponsible dad, will you take him?"

". . ."

Miss G. is still not looking at me; she's watching her flock, she just nods, but:

"On one condition," she whispers, without moving her lips.

"What?"

"That you don't expect me to thank you for it."

Oh, my terribly British Miss G., that silent consent is one of the most treasured memories I have of a teacher! It's in Marivaux, in Marivaux, do you hear? – not in one of your pious books, but in Marivaux! – that I found what is surely your secret motto: "In this world, you must be a bit too kind in order to be kind enough."

If I add that you got that boy all the way to his *bac*, I'll have said something about the results of such kindness.

2

All it takes is one teacher – just one – to save us from ourselves and make us forget all the others.

Or at least, that's how I remember Mr Bal.

He was our maths teacher when we were seventeen. His body language was the opposite of Keating's; you couldn't find a less film-friendly teacher: egg-shaped and with a high-pitched voice, no other distinguishing features. He would await us sitting at his desk, he would greet us in a friendly enough fashion, and his next words would propel us into the world of maths. So what did it consist of, this lesson that held us enthralled? Chiefly, the subject that Mr Bal was teaching, and which seemed to possess him, making him unusually vital, calm and kind. A strange goodness born of knowledge, of the natural desire to share with us the subject that delighted his mind, and which he could never have imagined our finding repulsive, or even strange. Bal was shaped by his subject and by his students. There was something of the village simpleton about him, a breathtaking innocence. The idea that his pupils might be unruly had clearly never crossed his mind, nor did it ever occur to us to tease him, so convincing was the pleasure he took in teaching.

Not that we were a docile audience. Nearly all of us had been rescued from the dustbin in Djibouti, and we were hardly endearing. I can remember a few nocturnal fights, in town, as well as scores settled in ways that were far from kind. But as soon as we walked through Mr Bal's door, it was as if we were purified by our immersion in mathematics, and, once the lesson was over, each of us would resurface as a *mathematikos*!

On the first day of class, with the most diehard no-hopers among us bragging about our zeros, he smiled and replied that he didn't believe in a mathematical set with nothing in it. Then he asked us several perfectly straightforward questions and pondered our elementary answers as if they were invaluable nuggets, which we found hilarious. And then he wrote the number twelve on the blackboard and asked us what he'd written.

The most resourceful tried to find a clever escape:

"The twelve fingers on a hand!"

"The twelve commandments!"

But his innocent smile proved a real disincentive.

"It's the minimum mark you'll get in your *bac*."

And he added: "If you stop being frightened."

Followed by: "And that's the last you'll hear from me on the subject. We're not here to concern ourselves with the *baccalauréat*, but with mathematics."

Sure enough, he never mentioned the *bac* again, not once. Metre by metre, he spent that year hauling us out of the abyss of our own ignorance, pretending that it was the very well of science; he always marvelled at what we knew, against all odds.

"You think you don't know anything, but you're mistaken, you know a huge amount! Look, Pennacchioni, did you know that you knew that?"

Of course, such maieutics wasn't enough to turn us into mathematical geniuses. Deep as our well might have been, though, Mr Bal hauled us all up to its rim: the pass mark for the *baccalauréat*.

And without ever alluding to the calamitous future which, according to so many teachers, had been lying in wait for us, and for so long.

3

Was Mr Bal himself a great mathematician? And, the year after, was Miss Gi a landmark historian? And, in my repeated final year, was Mr S. a peerless philosopher? I assume so, but the truth is I don't know; all I know is that the three of them had a passion for communicating their subjects. Armed with that passion, they tracked me down in the pit of my despondency and didn't give up until I had both feet planted firmly in their lessons, which proved to be the antechambers to my life. Not that they were any more interested in me than the others, no, they treated all students alike, good and bad; they simply knew how to rekindle the desire for learning. They supported our efforts step by step, celebrated our progress, weren't impatient with our slow-wittedness, never took our failures personally, and ensured that the rigorous demands they made of us were matched by the quality, consistency and generosity of their own work. You couldn't have imagined a more disparate group in every other way: Mr Bal, so calm and smiley, a mathematical Buddha; Miss Gi, a cone of air, a tornado that wrenched us from our straitjacket of laziness, dragging us into the tumultuous tunnel of History; Mr S., a sharp and sceptical philosopher (peaked nose, peaked hat, peaked belly), stationary and astute, who would leave me buzzing with questions as evening fell. I used to hand him bloated essays which he described as exceedingly thorough, thereby suggesting that, as a marker, he was accustomed to rather more concise homework.

On reflection, these three teachers had only one thing in common: they never gave up. They weren't easily taken in by our protestations of ignorance. (How many essays did Miss Gi make me rewrite due to my rickety spelling? How many extra lessons did Mr Bal give me because he found me in a corridor staring at nothing, or daydreaming in a study room? "How about a quick quarter of an hour of maths, Pennacchioni, since we're here? Come on, just fifteen minutes . . .") That gesture of saving a drowning person, that grip hauling you up despite your suicidal flailing, the raw, life-affirming image of a hand holding firmly on to a jacket collar is what first springs to mind when I think of them. In their presence – in their subjects – I gave birth to myself: a me who was a mathematician, a me who was an historian, a me who was a philosopher, a me who, in the space of an hour, forgot *myself* a bit, tucked myself between brackets, got rid of the me who, before encountering these teachers, had stopped me from feeling I was really there.

One other thing: I believe they all three had style. They were artists at conveying their subjects. Their lessons were feats of communication, of course, but of knowledge mastered to the point where it almost passed for spontaneous creation. Their ease transformed each lesson into an event to be remembered. As if Miss Gi were resuscitating history, Mr Bal rediscovering mathematics and Socrates speaking through Mr S.! They gave us lessons that were as memorable as the theorem, the peace treaty or the basic concept that constituted their subject on any particular day. Their teaching created *events*.

That's where their influence ended. Their apparent influence at least. They didn't try to make an impression on us beyond the subjects they embodied. They weren't the kind of teachers who took pride in influencing a group of adolescents in search of father figures. Did they even realize that their teaching was giving us our freedom? As for us, we were their mathematics, history or philosophy students, and that's all we were. Yes, we felt a certain pride as the members of an exclusive club, but they'd have been more surprised than anyone to learn that, forty-five years later, one of their students, who became a teacher thanks to them, would play the disciple to the point of erecting a statue to them! All the more so since, like my cellist from Blanc-Mesnil, once they'd gone home, they would hardly have given us another thought, aside from marking and lesson preparation. Of course, they must have had other interests, an open curiosity that fed their energy and which explained, among other things, their intense presence in the classroom. (Miss Gi, in particular, seemed to have an appetite for devouring the world and its libraries.) It wasn't just their knowledge that these teachers shared with us, it was the desire for knowledge itself. And what they communicated to me was a taste for passing it on. So we turned up to their lessons with hunger in our bellies. I wouldn't say that we felt liked by them, but we did feel well regarded (*not* "disrespected", as the youth of today would put it), a regard even apparent in the way they marked our homework, where their annotations were intended exclusively for the individual concerned. The model being the marking of Mr Beaum, our history teacher at *hypokhâgne*, who stipulated that we leave the last page of our essays blank, for him to type – in red, single-spaced – detailed corrections of our homework.

These teachers, encountered in my final years at school, were a great contrast to those who reduced their students to a common colourless mass, "this class", about which they only spoke using the superlatives of inferiority. We were always the worst year group of their careers; they'd never had a class *less* this . . . *more* that . . . You'd have thought that, year on year, they were teaching a public ever less worthy of their attention. They complained about the way the school was being run, about student meetings, about parents' evenings. Their whingeing aroused a ferocity in us akin to the rage of a drowning man as he drags down with him the cowardly captain who let the shipwrecked boat impale itself on the reef in the first place. (Alright, it's just an image . . . Let's say they were our ideal culprits, much as we were theirs; we defended ourselves against their routine depression by being wicked.)

The most fearsome among these was Mr Rebuking (a pseudonym), my wretched hangman when I was nine, who rained bad marks down on my head with such abandon that, to this day, if I'm stuck in some bureaucratic queue, I still think of the ticket I've been allocated as a judgement from Rebuking: "Number 175, Pennachioni, always near the bottom of the list!"

Then there was the science teacher in our final year, whom I have to thank for getting me expelled from my *lycée*. Bemoaning the fact that the average mark of "this class" was less than 3.5 out of 20, he was rash enough to ask us why. Eyebrows raised, chin tense, lips slack: "Well, can somebody explain this . . . prowess?"

I raised a polite index finger and suggested two possible explanations: either our class represented a monstrous statistic (thirty-two students who couldn't do any better than an average of 3.5 in biology), or else this scrawny result indicated the quality of teaching being dispensed.

Pleased with myself, I imagine.

And sent out of the classroom.

"Heroic but useless," a friend pointed out. "What's the difference between a teacher and a tool? . . . Give up? You can't mend a bad teacher."

So, expelled.

My father was furious, of course.

Dirty memories, those years of everyday resentment.

4

Instead of gathering and publishing the gems produced by dunces, which entertain so many staffrooms, we should create an anthology of good teachers. Literature has no shortage of such testimonials: Voltaire paying homage to the Jesuit fathers Tournemine and Porée; Rimbaud submitting his poems to his teacher Izambard; Camus writing filial letters to Mr Germain, his beloved primary-school teacher; Julien Green affectionately recalling the colourful Lesellier, his history teacher; Simone Weil singing the praises of her tutor Alain, who in turn never forgot how Jules Lagneau had whetted his own appetite for philosophy; J.-B. Pontalis celebrating Sartre, who "stood out" from all the other teachers . . .

If, in addition to those famous individuals, this anthology were to paint the portrait of the unforgettable teacher we've nearly all encountered at least once during our school careers, perhaps we'd be able to shed some light on the qualities necessary for practising this strange calling.

5

As far back as I can remember, when young teachers felt put off by a class, they complained about not having been properly prepared for "*this*". Today's *this,* which is all too real, covers areas as wide-ranging as dysfunctional families providing a poor upbringing, the sort of cultural damage linked to unemployment and exclusion, the loss of civic values that follows, violence, linguistic inequality and religiosity, as well as television and computer games – in short, everything that, in one way or another, fuels the diagnosis served up to us by the news each morning.

It is only one step from "We haven't been prepared for *this*" to "We're not here for *this*", which can also be expressed as: "We teachers aren't in school to resolve the social problems that impede the communication of knowledge; that's not our job. Provide us with enough supervisors, educationalists, social workers, psychologists – in short, specialists of every kind – and we can properly teach the subjects we have spent so many years studying." Wholly legitimate demands, in response to which minister after minister cites budgetary restrictions.

So we find ourselves in a new phase of training our teachers, one that will become increasingly focused on how we communicate with our students. Such an approach is vital, but if young teachers expect a normative discourse that will enable them to resolve all the problems likely to crop up in the classroom, they're headed for fresh disillusionment; the *this* for which they haven't been trained will resist such an approach. In a word, I fear that *this* might never let itself be altogether defined, that *this* might be nothing other than the sum of the elements that objectively constitute it.

6

The idea that you can teach without meeting any resistance relies on an idealized notion of the student. It would make sound pedagogical sense to hold up the dunce as the most normal student of all, the one who fully justifies the teacher's role, since he has *everything* to learn, starting with the importance of learning! Not a bit of it. Since the dawn of educational time, the student considered as normal has been the student who puts up the least resistance to teaching, the one who doesn't call our knowledge into question or put our competency to the test, a student who already knows a lot, who is gifted with instant comprehension, who spares us searching for the access roads to his grey matter, a student with a natural urge to learn, who can stop being a kid in turmoil or a teenager with problems during our lessons, a student convinced from the cradle that he has to curb his appetites and emotions by exercising his reason if he doesn't want to live in a jungle filled with predators, a student confident that the intellectual life is a source of infinite pleasures that can be refined to the extreme when most other pleasures are doomed to monotonous repetition – in short, a student who has understood that knowledge is the only answer: the answer to the slavery in which ignorance wants to keep us, the sole consolation for our ontological loneliness.

This is the heavenly picture of the ideal student that springs to mind when I hear the following statement: "I owe everything I am to the French education system." I'm not calling the speaker's gratitude into question here. "My father was a labourer, and I owe everything to state education!" Nor am I playing down the merits of school. "I'm the son of an immigrant, and I owe everything to state education!"

I can't help it: as soon as I hear this public manifestation of gratitude, I can see a film starting – feature-length – glorifying school, yes, but above all glorifying this child who understood, from his very first lesson at nursery school, that the state was ready to guarantee him a future as long as he was the student that the educational system expected him to be. Shame on those who didn't live up to such expectations! At which point a voice starts whispering the film's commentary inside my head:

"You're right, my friend, you owe a great deal to your state education, an enormous amount even, but not everything; there you're wrong. You're forgetting the vagaries of chance. Perhaps you were more gifted than the average child, for example. Or a young immigrant raised by loving parents who were determined and smart, like the parents of my friend Kahina, who wanted their three daughters to be independent graduates so that no man would ever treat them the way the women of their own generation had been treated. On the other hand, you may be the product of a family tragedy, like my old friend Pierre, and, finding your only salvation in studying, you may have dived in deeply to forget – for as long as the lesson lasted – what was going on at home. Then again, you may have been a child imprisoned in an asthmatic cage, like Minne, thirsty to learn everything straight away in order to escape the sickbed: "Learning meant breathing," she tells me, "it was like opening a window, learning so as not to feel choked, learning, reading, writing, breathing, always opening more windows, give me air, give me air, I swear, schoolwork was the only way to escape my asthma, and I didn't really care about how good the teachers were, getting out of bed, going to school, counting, multiplying, dividing, learning the rule of three, applying Mendel's laws, knowing a little more every day, that's all I wanted, to breathe, more air, give me more air!" Or you may have been gifted with the flippant megalomania of Jérôme: "As soon as I learned to read and count, I knew the world was mine! When I was ten, I spent the weekends at my grandmother's hotel, and, on the pretext of helping out in the dining room, I pestered the guests by setting them all sorts of teasers: How old was Louis XIV when he died? What's a predictive adjective? A hundred-and-twenty-three times seventy-two? My favourite answer was: I've got no idea, but you're going to tell me. It was funny to know more, aged ten, than the local pharmacist or curate! They patted my cheek when in fact they wanted to pull my head off, which I thought was hilarious."

"Excellent students, Kahina, Minne, Pierre, Jérôme, and you, and you, as well as my friend Françoise, who learned by playing, beginning when she was very small, without any inhibitions – Wow! Her staggering capacity for serious fun! – to the point that she sat her *agrégation* in Classics as if she was playing *Le Jeu des Mille Euros* on the radio. The sons and daughters of immigrants, labourers, office workers, technicians, primary-school teachers and the upper middle classes, these friends are so different from one another, but excellent students every one of them. The least our education system could do was to spot you, and you, and you! And to help you become the people you are. For it to fail you, now that would have been the limit. Our education system leaves more than enough casualties by the roadside, wouldn't you say?

"By appearing to hold school in such high regard, it's actually yourself you're flattering; whether consciously or not, you're holding yourself up as the ideal student. And in so doing, you mask the countless factors that make us so unequal in our acquisition of knowledge: personal circumstances, family circumstances, pathology, temperament . . . Oh yes, the mystery of temperament.

"'I owe everything to state education!'

"Might it be that you want to pass off your natural ability as a virtue? (They're not incompatible, by the way . . .) To reduce your success to a matter of determination, tenacity and sacrifice, is that what you want? You're right to point out that you were a hard-working student who persevered, credit where credit's due; but this is also about the pleasure you took, from very early on, in your ability to understand, about the great joy, following your first encounters with school work, of having understood, of knowing that your effort held the promise of that joy! As I was sitting down at my desk, crushed by my own belief in how stupid I was, you were settling at yours, quivering with impatience, because you wanted to move on to the next thing, for, in a flash, you could dispatch the same maths problem I was falling asleep over. Homework was the springboard of your mind but also the shifting sands where mine foundered. It left you as free as air, with the satisfaction of a mission accomplished, and me dazed by ignorance, trying to pass off a sketchy draft as a final version with the help of carefully drawn lines that didn't fool anybody. From the outset, you were the worker, I was the lazybones. So that's what laziness meant? This foundering within oneself? And what did work mean? How did those who worked well set about it? Where did their strength come from? This was the mystery of my childhood. The same effort that broke me was, you realized, the forfeit to be paid in order to blossom later on. You and I didn't know that 'you have to succeed to understand', as Piaget put it, and that you, like me, were the living illustration of that maxim.

"You've kept this passion for understanding alive all your life, and you've done a good job of it. That determination still sparkles in your eyes! Only a jealous fool would begrudge you it. But please stop trying to pass off your natural ability as a virtue; it clouds the issue, it complicates the already highly complex question of education (and is rather a widespread character flaw).

"Do you know what you really were?

"You were icing-on-the-cake students."

That was what, when I became a teacher myself, I used to call (*in petto*) my top students, those rare gems, when I found one in my class. I was very fond of my icing-on-the-cake students! They provided a respite from the others. And they stimulated me. The one who twigs quickest, gives the most spot-on answers, and often wittily so, that eye lighting up, that relaxed discretion which is the supreme grace of intelligence. Little Noémie, for example (sorry, big Noémie – she's seventeen now!), thanked last year by her French teacher on her school report: "Thank you," it read, just "Thank you". He was clean out of eulogistic appreciation: *Noémie P., French 19/20, Thank you.* That's justice for you: state education owes a lot to Noémie. As it does to my young cousin

Pierre, who told us he got top marks in his *bac*, before heading off in the early days of July 2007 to face a particularly irascible ocean on a sailing boat: "Give me a bigger adventure than exams . . ." his handsome smile seemed to say.

Yes, I've always liked good students.

And felt sorry for them, too. Because they have their own struggles: never disappointing adults, being irked by coming second when that idiot so-and-so monopolizes first place, detecting teachers' limits in lessons not quite nailed, and so getting slightly bored in class, enduring the mockery or jealousy of the dunces, weathering accusations of sucking up to authority – to which can be added, as for everybody, the usual confusion of growing up.

Portrait of an icing-on-the-cake student: Philippe, first year of *collège*, circa 1975, lanky eleven-year-old Philippe, with jug ears and an enormous orthodontic brace that makes him lisp like a bee. I ask him if he's fully grasped the notion of literal vs figurative language, about which we've just been talking.

"Literal and figurative language? Abtholutely, thir! I can think of plenty of exampleth!"

"Go ahead, Philippe, we're all ears."

"So, yetherday evening we had gueths round. My mother introduced me in figurative language. She thaid: 'Thith ith Philippe, our youngeth little one.' Now, it'th true I'm the youngeth, for the time being anyway, but I'm thertainly not little; in fact I'm big for my age! 'He eath like a thparrow.' That'th a stupid exthprethon; birdth are meant to eat their own body weight in food every day, and I eat hardly anything. Then she thaid I alwayth had my head in the cloudth, when my head wath right there, at the table, for everybody to thee. But when she thpoke to me, it wath in literal language: 'Be quiet, wipe your mouth, don't put your elbowth on the table, thay goodnight and go to bed now . . .'"

Philippe concluded from this that figurative language was used by hostesses and literal language by mothers.

"And by teacherth, thir," he elaborated, "by teacherth talking to their studenth!"

I don't know what's become of my lisping Philippe, the archetypal icing-on-the-cake student. How does he spend his days? As a teacher? I'd like it if that were the case. Or, better, at *Normale Sup* or at a teacher training college, where his job is to equip teachers to deal with students as they really are. Perhaps he's lost his gift for pedagogy. Perhaps he was thought too inventive to teach, perhaps he fell by the wayside, perhaps he took off . . .

7

So, the student as he or she really is: that's what it's all about.

"Watch out," my friends warned me when I started writing this book, "students have changed a great deal since your childhood, even in the dozen years since you stopped teaching. They're really not the same any more, you know!"

Yes and no.

Today's children and teenagers are the same ages I was at the end of the '50s – that, at least, is something we share. They have to get up just as early, their timetables and rucksacks are just as heavy, and their teachers, good or bad, are still the dish of choice on the menu of their conversations – that makes three other points we have in common.

But here's a difference! There are more of them than there were in my childhood, when for many students school ended when they got their school certificates. And they're of every colour, at least in my neighbourhood, where the residents are the immigrants who've built contemporary Paris. Numbers and colours make for noteworthy differences, yes, but ones that fade the moment you leave the 20th *arrondissement*, especially differences of colour. There are fewer and fewer of them, students of colour, as you head down our hills towards the centre of Paris. Barely any in the *lycées* that flank the Panthéon. Very few black or *beur* students in our city centres – what you might call a charitable proportion – there we're back in the white schools of the 1960s.

No, the fundamental difference between the students of today and those of yesterday lies somewhere else: *they don't wear their big brothers' cast-offs*. That's the real difference! My mother would knit a pullover for Bernard, who, once he'd grown out of it, would pass it on to me. The same went for Doumé and Jean-Louis, our older brothers. Our mother's "thick woollies" were our predictable Christmas surprises. And despite most of the children of my generation wearing them, there was no brand name, no *pull Maman* label.

Not today. Today, Granny Marketing dresses everybody, big and small. She dresses, feeds, quenches their thirst, provides shoes, styles hair, kits everyone out; she bedecks the student with electronic devices, mounts him on roller blades, a bicycle, a moped, a motorbike, a scooter; she entertains him, informs him, plugs him in, has him in a state of permanent musical transfusion and scatters him to the four corners of the consumable universe; she's the one who sends him to sleep; she's the one who wakes him up; and, when he sits down in class, she's the one who vibrates in his pocket to reassure him: I'm here, don't be afraid, I'm here, in your phone, you're not a hostage in the ghetto of school!

8

A child died, in the '70s. Let's call that child Jules, after Jules Ferry, minister for education between 1878 and 1883. We behave as if the child Jules was immortal, had been around forever, but he was only conceived a century or so ago, and I'm shocked to realize that he hasn't lasted as long as my aged mother. Dreamt up by Rousseau around 1760, in the form of a prototype called Émile, he was brought into being a century later by Victor Hugo, who made it his task to free children from the work to which the nascent industrial world had chained them: "The right of every child is to become a man," Hugo wrote in *Things Seen*; "what makes the man is light; what makes the light is education. Therefore, free and compulsory education is the right of every child."

At the end of the 1870s, the French Republic made this child sit on the benches of a school that was secular, free and compulsory, so that his fundamental needs might be satisfied: reading, writing, counting, thinking, turning himself into a citizen conscious of his individual and national identities. The child Jules wore two hats: he was a schoolboy in class and a son at home. His family was responsible for raising him, the school for educating him. These two worlds were practically sealed off from each other, as was the universe of the child Jules: he experienced the terrifying burgeoning of adolescence without having any information to go on; he got lost in conjectures about the female sex, imagining a great deal and correcting his imagination with the means available to him; as for his games, most of them relied entirely on his powers of imagination. Exceptional cases apart, the child Jules played no part in the emotional, economic and professional concerns of grown-ups. He was neither a worker in society, nor someone the family confided in, nor a person with whom his teachers discussed ideas. Naturally, as with all worlds, this corseted society was simple in appearance only; sentiment infiltrated it through any number of cracks, giving it human complexity. But the fact remains that the rights of the child Jules were limited to his education and his duties of being a good son, a good student and, should it arise, a good corpse: out of an army of six million Juleses, one million three hundred and fifty thousand were massacred between 1914 and 1918, and most of the rest failed to return home in one piece.

The child Jules lived for a hundred years.

1875–1975.

Broadly speaking.

Plucked out of industrial society in the last quarter of the nineteenth century, a hundred years later he was dropped into consumer society, which made him into a child customer.

9

There are five sorts of children on our planet today: the child customer in our own society, the child producer under different skies, elsewhere the child soldier, the child prostitute and, on the curved adverts in the *métro*, the dying child whose image, periodically, looms over our jadedness looking hungry and abandoned.

Children, all five of them.

Exploited, all five of them.

10

Child customers include those who have parental income at their disposal and those who don't; those who buy and those who get by. In both scenarios, money rarely being the product of work personally undertaken, the young acquirer becomes the owner of property he hasn't paid for. That's what a child customer is: a child who, across a range of consumer areas which are *identical to those of his parents or his teachers* (clothing, food, phones, music, electronic goods, travel, leisure activities . . .), becomes a property owner without much opposition.

In so doing, he plays the same economic role as the adults responsible for his upbringing and education. Like them, he constitutes an enormous chunk of the market, like them he makes the currency go round (the fact that it's not his doesn't matter); his desires, as much as those of his parents, must endlessly be courted and renewed to keep the engine ticking over. Seen from this perspective, he's someone important: a customer in his own right. Just like the grown-ups.

An independent consumer.

From his first childish desires.

And satisfying those desires becomes a way of measuring the love we feel for him.

Try as they might to defend themselves, grown-ups can't do much about this. That's how the market economy works: loving your child (this child, who's so *wished for* in our part of the world that its birth digs a bottomless debt of love for its parents) means loving its desires, which are soon expressed as vital needs: the need for love and the desire for objects become one and the same, since the proof of that love lies in purchasing those objects.

The child's desires . . .

There you go, another difference between today's child and myself, back then: was I a *wished for* child?

Loved, yes, in the manner of my bygone era, but wished for?

What a face she'd pull, my old mother, whose 101st birthday we've just celebrated (I'm obviously writing this book too slowly), if I asked her: "By the way, mother dearest, did you really want me?"

" . . . ?"

"Yes, you heard me: was I expressly wished for by you, by Father, by both of you?"

I can imagine her gaze coming to rest on me. I can hear the long silence that follows. And then, a question for a question: "Tell me, did you come good in the end?"

If I dug a bit deeper, I might eventually get a few details:

"It was the war, your father was on leave, he took us to Casablanca, your three brothers and me, so he could join the United States Army of Europe in Provence. You were born in Casablanca."

Or even, like a good southern mother: "I was a bit worried you might be a girl; I've always preferred boys."

But finding out whether I was wanted: no. There was an adjective to qualify those kinds of questions in my family, at that time: they were *ludicrous.*

Right, back to the child customer.

Let's put things in perspective: in describing him, I'm not seeking to present him as a despicable brainwashed sybarite, nor am I preaching a return to *pull Maman,* to tin toys, darned socks, family silences, the Ogino method and everything else that makes today's youth think of ours as if it was a black-and-white film. No, I simply wonder what sort of dunce I'd have been if, let's say, I'd been born fifteen years ago. No doubt about it: I'd have been a dunce consumer. Not being intellectually precocious, I'd have made do with commercial maturity, which confers on teenage desires the same legitimacy as on those of their parents. I'd have made this a matter of principle. I can just hear myself: you've got your computer, so I've got *a right* to one of my own! Especially if you don't want me to touch yours! And they would have given in. Out of love. Love gone off the rails? It's easy to say so. Each era imposes its own language on familial love. Ours prescribes the language of objects. Don't forget the diagnosis of Granny Marketing: "His identity's at stake." Like a good number of children and teenagers I hear everywhere I go, I'd have known how to convince my mother that conforming to the group depended on such and such a purchase, as did my personal well-being: "Mum, I've just got to have the latest N.'s!"

Would my mother have wanted me to be a pariah? Weren't my abominable school results bad enough? Did we really need to make things any worse?

"Mum, I swear, or else I'll look like a nerd!" (Correction: "nerd" is a bit dated). "I'll look like a geek, and that's like, *no way!*" (In his time, Michel Audiard would have said "twerp" or "sucker"). "Mum, if you don't get me these trainers, they'll think I'm a twerp!")

And my loving mother would have caved in.

Except that, fifteen years ago, would I have been the last-born of four brothers? Would my parents have *wished for* me? Would they even have allowed me to come into this world?

It all comes down to a question of budget, just like everything else.

II

One of the aspects of "*this*" – for which today's young teacher hasn't been prepared – is facing a classroom of child customers head-on. Yes, he was one himself, as indeed are his own children, but in this classroom he's a teacher. And as a teacher, he doesn't feel the debt of love that stirs his fatherly heart. The student is not a *wished for* child who has the teaching profession melting with gratitude. We're at primary school, *collège* or *lycée* here, not at home or in a shopping mall: we're not gratifying superficial desires with presents, we're satisfying fundamental needs with responsibilities. The need to get an education is all the more difficult to meet when it must first be awakened. It's a tough task for the teacher, this conflict between desires and needs. And a painful outlook for the young customer busying himself with his needs at the cost of his desires: having to empty his head in order to shape his mind, to unplug himself in order to connect with knowledge, to swap the pseudo-ubiquity of machines for the universality of understanding, to forget flashy clutter in order to take in invisible abstractions. The ultimate insult being that he has to pay with his person for this educational knowledge whereas satisfying his desires doesn't commit him in any way. For the paradox of free education, as inherited from Jules Ferry, is that today's state education system remains the last place in a market economy where the child customer must *pay with his or her own being*, and abide by a strict *quid pro quo*: work for knowledge, effort for understanding, the solitary practice of reflection for access to universality, being fully present at school for a vague promise of a future – this is what school demands.

If the good student, who has a natural ability to make allowances, is satisfied with this state of affairs, why would the dunce accept it? Why would he give up the prestige of commercial maturity for the position of an obedient student, which feels condescending to him? In a society where sham knowledge, in the guise of thrills and interaction, is freely on offer from morning to night, why would he go to school to pay for the real thing? For all that he may be a dunce in class, isn't he master of the universe when, shut away in his bedroom, he's sitting in front of his games console? Chatting into the small hours, isn't he communicating with the whole world? Doesn't his keyboard promise him access to anyone he might desire? Don't his battles against virtual armies offer him a thrilling life? Why would he trade this command-and-control position for a chair in a classroom? Why would he endure the disapproval of adults scrutinizing his end-of-term report when, locked in his bedroom, cut off from family and school, he is master of all he surveys?

There's no doubt about it: if the dunce I was had been born fifteen years ago, and if his mother hadn't given in to his every whim, he'd have plundered the family safe, but this time in order to buy gifts for himself! He'd have given himself the latest model of escapism, let himself be sucked into his computer, cut loose in order to surf space-time, no limits and no constraints, no schedule and no horizon, he'd have chatted with other versions of himself, no goals, no arguments. He'd have loved this era, which, despite not offering a future to its bad students, is prodigal with machines for abolishing their present. He'd have been the ideal prey for a society that excels at manufacturing obese young people by disembodying them.

12

"Me, an obese, disembodied young person?"

(Good God, there he is again . . .)

"Who said you could speak for me?"

Hell's bells! Why did I conjure him up, this dunce I used to be, this hopelessly dumb memory of myself? Here I am, in the home stretch at last; he'd left me in peace since that conversation about Maximilien, and now here he is again.

"Answer me! What gives you the right to think that if I'd been born fifteen years ago, I'd have turned into the hyper-consuming dunce you've been describing?"

No doubt about it; it's him alright. Always demanding explanations instead of delivering results. Right, here we go:

"Since when did I need your permission to write anything?"

"Since you started pontificating about dunces! The way I see it, when it comes to dunces *I'm* the expert!"

Are we experts in what we suffer from? Should sick people replace quacks and bad students be substituted for their teachers? There's no point in provoking him; he's quite capable of making me blacken pages on the subject. Let's get it over with as quickly as we can.

"Alright. What kind of dunce do *you* think you'd be today?"

"For all I know, I'd be doing just fine, thank you. School isn't the only thing in life, you know! You've been boring us from the start with school, but there are other solutions. You've got loads of friends who've been highly successful outside of school. That needs saying, too. Look at Bertrand, Robert, Mike and Françoise: they all left school early and they've done more than alright. They've made very nice lives for themselves, haven't they? So why not me? Who knows, I might have become an I.T. whizz by now!"

"..."

"No? Does that prospect bother you when you can barely turn on a computer? You want me to be a dunce, don't you, through and through? And a safe-breaker. All to prove a point? Alright then. If I'd been born fifteen years ago, I would have been a dunce, the worst in your class, and you'd never have stopped moaning: 'I wasn't trained for *this*, I wasn't trained for *this*.' Isn't that how you see it?"

"..."

"In any case, the question isn't what I would or wouldn't have been."

"Then what is the question?"

"The true nature of *this*, which young teachers declare they haven't been trained for; that's the only question, and you asked it yourself."

"Answer?"

"It's as old as the hills: teachers aren't prepared for the collision between knowledge and ignorance. And that's that!"

"Whatever you say."

"Too right. These stories about people losing their grip, about violence and consumerism, all that waffle is just the explanation *du jour*; tomorrow it'll be something else. Anyway, you said it yourself: the true nature of *this* can't be reduced to the sum of elements that objectively constitute it."

"Which doesn't shed any light on what it is."

"I've just told you: the clash of knowledge and ignorance! It's too violent. There you go, that's the true nature of *this.* Aren't you listening to me?"

"I'm listening, I'm listening."

I listen and he launches with teacherly authority into the well-oiled lesson, standing before his imaginary class – he couldn't be more self-assured – again putting forward, if I understand rightly, the argument that the true nature of *this* lies in the eternal conflict between knowledge as it conceives of itself and ignorance as it is lived: the abject failure of teachers to understand the state of ignorance in which their dunces stew, because they themselves were good students, at least in the subjects they teach. Teachers' great handicap lies in their failure to imagine themselves *not knowing what they know.* Whatever difficulties they may have experienced in acquiring their knowledge, once acquired it becomes part of them; they perceive it as obvious ("But it's *obvious*, come on!"), and they can't imagine how alien it seems to those who, in this particular field, exist in a state of ignorance.

"You, for example, who took a whole year to learn the letter *A*, can you, today, imagine yourself not being able to read or write? No! No more than a maths teacher could imagine himself not knowing that two and two make four. Well, there was a time when you couldn't read. You were just wading about in the alphabet. Pathetic is what you were! Do you remember Djibouti? May I remind you of the time, not so long ago, when you felt that Alice, your daughter – today a greater reader than you – was showing unwilling at reading the books that school plonked in front of her? Fool! Unworthy father! You'd forgotten that you yourself had experienced the same difficulty. And that you were infinitely slower than your daughter in this regard. But once you'd become a grown-up who *knew things*, Sir proved impatient with a kid who was trying to learn. As an informed teacher and concerned father, you'd quite simply lost your sense of ignorance!"

I'm listening, I'm listening. When he's moving at this rate of speed, I know there's no stopping him.

"You teachers are all the same! What you need are lessons in ignorance. You put yourselves through all sorts of exams and competitions in your specialisms, when your most important quality should be your ability to understand *what it feels like to be the person who doesn't know what you know*! I dream of a test for the *Capès* or the *agreg* in which the candidate would be asked to remember a time when he'd failed at school – a sudden nosedive in maths, for example, when he was fifteen or sixteen – and to describe what happened to him that year."

"Well, he'd blame his teacher."

"Not good enough! Teacher's fault, I know all about that, I used to say it myself. No, the candidates would be asked to dig deeper, to find out why they'd really come unstuck that year. To look inside themselves, and outside themselves, into their heads, into their hearts, into their bodies, into their neurons, into their hormones, to look everywhere. And to remember how they escaped. The methods they used. Those famous inner strengths. Where were those strengths hiding? What did they look like? I'd go further: apprentice teachers should be asked why they've dedicated themselves to one subject rather than another. Why teach English and not maths or history? Simply a matter of choice? Well, let them rummage around in those subjects they didn't choose. Let them remember their weak points in physics, how hopeless they were at philosophy, their stupid excuses in P.E. In short, those who claim to teach must have a clear view of their own experience at school. Let them *feel* what ignorance is like, a little, if they want to have the slightest chance of helping us escape from it."

"If I've understood properly, you're suggesting that teachers should be recruited from bad students rather than good ones?"

"Why not? If they've come out the other side but can remember the students they used to be, why not? After all, you owe me a lot!"

". . ."

"Don't you?"

". . ."

"Don't you? As far as teaching goes, I reckon you owe me big-time. You needed to be a dunce in order to become a teacher, didn't you? Be honest. If you'd shone in class, you'd have done something else. As it is, you went back to the dustbin in Djibouti, disguised as a teacher, to help get the other dunces out. And it's thanks to me that you succeeded. Because you knew what I'd been through. That's *knowledge* of a kind, don't you think?"

(If he imagines I'm going to give him the pleasure . . .)

"Let me tell you what I think: that you're getting on our nerves with this empathy business, and that it would irritate more than one teacher. If you'd taken yourself in hand once and for all, you'd have made it through on your own."

Now he really blows his top. At first, because he doesn't understand the word *empathy*, then, once it's been explained to him, because he understands it only too well.

"Not empathy! Who cares about your empathy? It'd sink us, your empathy! Nobody's asking you to put yourself in our shoes; we're asking you to save those kids who can't ask on their own behalf, don't you understand? We're asking you to add an intuitive understanding of ignorance to your vast knowledge, to go fishing for dunces, because that's your job! The bad student will take himself in hand when you've taught him how to take himself in hand. That's all we ask!"

"Who's *we*?"

"Me!"

"Ah, you . . . And what do you have to say, Mr Expert, about the condition of being ignorant?"

"I'd say that it's not the black hole you imagine it to be. In fact, it's quite the opposite. It's a flea market where you can find anything and everything *except* the desire to learn what teachers are teaching. The bad student never sees himself as ignorant. Take me. I never thought of myself as ignorant, I thought I was stupid; there's a big difference! The dunce sees himself as unworthy, or abnormal, or rebellious, or else he couldn't care less; he sees himself as knowing a whole heap of things, just not what you're claiming to teach him, but he doesn't see himself as being ignorant of what you know. Soon he doesn't want anything more to do with your knowledge. He's kissed it goodbye. His bereavement might be painful, but what can I say? He's more involved in keeping the pain alive than in trying to heal it; this may be hard to understand, but that's how it is. He mistakes his ignorance for his true nature. He's not a *maths student*, but a *maths no-hoper*; that's how it is. Seeing as he needs to compensate for this, he'll shine in other areas. As a safe-breaker, in my case. And as an occasional face-puncher. And when he gets nicked by the police, when the social worker asks him why he isn't keeping up his studies, do you know what he says?"

". . ."

"*Exactly the same thing as the teacher: this*, yes, *this* again! We weren't meant to be, school and me; I'm not made for *this*, that's what he says. Without realizing it, he too is talking about the dreadful clash between ignorance and knowledge. It's the same *this* as the teachers' *this*. Teachers reckon they haven't been trained to cope with the kinds of students they find in their classes, who in turn reckon they're not meant to be there. From both sides, the same *this*!

"So how do we remedy *this*, if empathy is discouraged?"

Long pause.

I press him: "Come on, since you know everything without having learned anything, is there a *way* to teach without being prepared for it? Is there a method?"

"Methods aren't what's missing here; in fact methods are all we've got. You spend your time hiding behind methods when deep down you know perfectly well that no method is sufficient. No, what's missing is something else."

"What?"

"I can't say it."

"Why?"

"It's a rude word."

"Worse than *empathy*?"

"No comparison. A word you absolutely can't say in a primary school, a *lycée*, a university or anywhere like that."

"Tell us?"

"No, really, I can't . . ."

"Oh, go on!"

"I'm telling you, I can't. If you use this word when talking about education, you'll be lynched."

"..."

"..."

"..."

"It's *love.*"

13

It's true that our society frowns upon talking about love in the context of teaching. Try it and see. You might as well talk about rope in a hanged man's house.

We're better off resorting to metaphor when it comes to describing the kind of love that drives Miss G., Nicole H., the teachers I've written about in these pages, most of those who invite me into their classrooms, all the tireless teachers out there I haven't met.

So, a metaphor.

A winged metaphor, as it happens.

Vercors again.

One morning last September.

The very first days of September.

I fall asleep working on some page or other of this book late into the night. I awake impatient to pick up where I left off. I'm about to leap out of bed when a subtle racket stops me. Cheeping all around the house. Countless chirrupings, intense but sustained. Ah, yes, the swallows are leaving! Every year around the same date, they arrange to meet on the electricity cables. Fields and roadsides are covered in musical scores, as on a cheap greetings card. They're getting ready to migrate. The hullabaloo of reunions. Those flying around seek permission to fall into line from those already on the cables; they're all quivering with desire for the horizon. Hurry, we're off! We're coming, we're coming!

They fly at top speed. From the north, in Hitchcockian battalions, heading south. And this is the exact orientation of our bedroom: north–south. A skylight to the north, a double window to the south. Each year the same drama: tricked by the transparency of these perfectly aligned windows, a fair number of swallows crash into the skylight.

No writing this morning, then. I open the north-facing skylight and the south-facing double window, I dive back into our bed; our morning will be made over to watching squadrons of swallows traversing our bedroom, silent all of a sudden, intimidated perhaps by these two people lying in bed inspecting them. Except that, on either side of the double window, a thin vertical glass pane remains shut. There's a huge space between the two fixed panes, big enough for all the birds in the sky to pass through. Yet it always happens: three or four of the idiots fly straight into the fixed panes. Our proportion of dunces. Our deviants. They're not in line. They're not following the path. They're larking about on the edge. Result: fixed pane. Whack! Stunned on the carpet. At which point, one of us gets up, picks up the stunned swallow – they weigh hardly anything, with their bones of wind – waits for it to wake up again and sends it back out to join its friends. The resuscitated bird flies off, still a bit groggy, zigzagging across reclaimed space, then it darts south in a straight line and disappears into its future.

There you go: take my metaphor for what it's worth, but that's what I believe love looks like, in the context of teaching, when our students fly like crazed birds. This is what Miss G. and Nicole H. have dedicated their lives to: releasing a flight of crashed swallows from their educational comas. We don't always succeed; sometimes we fail to show the way, some of them don't wake up, they remain on the carpet or break their necks against another pane; they settle in our consciences like those holes of regret where the dead swallows lie at the bottom of our garden. But every time we try, we will have tried. They are *our* students. Questions of sympathy or antipathy towards this one or that one (and very real questions they are too!) don't come into it. Good luck to anyone who can decipher our feelings for them. Neither affection nor sentiment is at stake here. It's a matter of life and death. A stunned swallow is a swallow to be brought back to life. Full stop.

Translator's Note

Making a work that is firmly located in the educational system of one country accessible to the readers of another country is always a challenge for the translator. The educational "blues" that Daniel Pennac experienced as a student – and from which, as a teacher, he rescued students – may be universal, but the system in which these blues are played out is specifically French. I hope the following overview will guide the reader through some of the system's intricacies, not to mention the pitfalls of translating it.

French schooling divides into four stages: *école maternelle* (nursery school, ages three–six); *école élémentaire* (primary school, six–eleven); *collège* (secondary school, eleven–fifteen); and *lycée* (sixth-form college, fifteen–eighteen). I have referred to students by the average age of their year-group rather than by the name assigned to that year-group, since such classifications are subject to change.

Pennac refers to a school career haunted by the threat of having to "repeat" or be "kept down" a year. This prospect of *redoublement* is all too real in French schools. From *collège* onwards, it applies to those students who consistently fail to make the grade in a marking system scored out of *20*. For teachers and parents to keep tabs on students, and to communicate with each other about daily school business, including absences, there is the *carnet de correspondance* (notebook) which students take to school every day.

The *school certificate* that Pennac's Uncle Jules attempted to get his Corsican schoolchildren to pass was the leaving certificate taken at the end of primary school; formerly, this was the basic school-leaving qualification. The B.E.P.C. (secondary-school diploma) is now sat at fifteen and is roughly equivalent to G.C.S.E.s or Scottish Highers. It marks the end of a student's time at *collège* and helps determine the kind of *lycée* to which he or she will progress, including whether academic or more technical. At an academic *lycée*, the focus is on passing the *baccalauréat*, or *bac*, in the final year. This examination is taken to A-level standard, though with a much broader subject base.

The cream of the Parisian crop might be primed from birth for a place at *Louis-le-Grand*, not just a highly competitive *lycée* but also a feeder or prep school for the *grandes écoles* (alumni include Molière, Voltaire, Hugo and all the presidents of the Fifth Republic with the exception of Sarkozy). Here, after the *bac*, students cram for the fiercely competitive entrance exams to the *grandes écoles*. Given the high-pressure nature of this preparation, the nickname for the first year of humanities cramming is ironic, to say the least: *hypokhâgne*, from *cagne*, "laziness".

The *grandes écoles* are elite higher-education establishments (as opposed to the open-entry universities), many of which were dreamt up during the French Revolution. The most prestigious include:

- the *Ecole Polytechnique* (engineering), whose alumni are known as *polytechniciens*;
- the four *Ecoles Normales Supérieures* (E.N.S.), originally founded to train teachers for the *agrégation* (competitive exam for top teaching positions); alumni present and past – including, famously, Jean-Paul Sartre – are known as *normaliens*;
- the *Ecole Normale d'Administration* (E.N.A.), the training ground for the civil service; alumni are known as *énarques.*

Despite a brief stint in *hypokhâgne*, Pennac himself decided to steer clear of both the *agrégation* and the *capès* – the latter being a P.G.C.E. equivalent for aspirant secondary-school teachers who have gained a university degree.

The language in *Chagrin d'école* is breathtakingly wide-ranging: obstinately archaic one moment, savvily up-to-the-minute the next, but consistently alight with wit and humanity. When the choice of vocabulary is old-fashioned, there is always a reason behind it. So when Pennac designates the *maîtres*, or schoolmasters, of his youth, he is echoing the tone of his formative years rather than using the more contemporary *profs*. Endeavouring to capture his deceptive simplicity of tone has sometimes meant erring towards a more modern or accessible lexicon. For example, Pennac was a teenager at roughly the time when the concept of being one was just entering popular culture and parlance (though the French still refer to *l'adolescence*, and to being an *ado*); his tone is so light that it seems to make sense to have him describe himself variously as one or the other.

Grammar and wordplay present similar challenges, especially as English grammar is no longer taught in the strict way that French grammar is taught in French schools, where the conjugation of verbs, recognition of *verb groups* (*-er*, *-ir*, *-re* etc.) is all par for the course. When Pennac goes to his dictionary to find out whether *meuf*, *keuf* and *teuf* have made an official entry into the French language, he is dealing with *verlan*, or back-slang, which involves splicing and reversing words or their segments. *Verlan* is the playful, defiant language of France's high-rise suburbs (*banlieues*) with their large immigrant and low-income communities. Although there is an improvised aspect to this wordplay, it is also systematic enough for words to filter through to the mainstream. Which is why *meuf*, *keuf* and *teuf* crop up in Pennac's dictionary. As, I suspect, would *beur*, back-slang for *arabe* (used to refer to a second- or third-generation French national of North African origin).

In Part 5, Pennac refers to Maximilien as the face of the contemporary dunce, describing him as a teenager who lives in a high-rise outside the urban ring road, or *périphérique*. The *banlieue* is largely beyond the reach of the *métro*, and is served instead by the *R.E.R.*, or Paris-region overground express trains. Maximilien, Pennac tells us, might be black, *beur* or *relegated Gaul*, a playful reference to France's World Cup-winning football team of 1998, dubbed *black-blanc-beur* rather than the conventional *bleu-blanc-rouge* of the French flag. Another phrase associated both with Maximilien and the *banlieues* is "*avoir la haine*", made famous by Mathieu Kassovitz's film *La Haine* (1995). The expression literally means "to feel full of hatred", in the sense of fuming with violent anger, though there is also a latent sense of being on the sharp end of other people's contempt.

Finally, in Part 4, one of the words Pennac traces is *vache*, for "cow", which is the root of both *vacherie* and *vachement*. The latter weighs in as the equivalent of "bloody", and the former refers to a nasty trick, general meanness or a below-the-belt remark: rather more pointed than, say, the English insult of calling someone a "silly old cow".

Glossary

page 4 ROBERT *Le Petit Robert des noms propres* (dictionary of proper nouns), otherwise known as *Le Petit Robert 2*, is the encyclopaedic complement to the language dictionary *Le Petit Robert*.

page 5 BERNARD PIVOT (born 1935) Hugely influential journalist, interviewer and host of French cultural television programmes. Most significantly, Pivot hosted *Apostrophes*, broadcast between 1975 and 1990. This literary programme, with six invited authors facing first Pivot's and then each other's questions, brought serious fiction to a mass audience and had a significant impact on book sales.

page 14 EMIL CIORAN (1911–1995) Romanian philosopher and essayist.

page 14 JULES FERRY (1832–1893) French statesman of the Third Republic, who twice served briefly as prime minister. Best known for his government's establishment of free, secular and compulsory primary education, his policy also involved anti-clerical measures. From 1880, girls were also able to benefit from a state secondary education.

page 15 LA COUR DES COMPTES Civil-service financial auditing body, responsible for controlling and regulating the accounts of state and state-owned institutions and companies, as well as the social security system and private organizations in receipt of public funding.

page 20 RENAUD (born 1952) French protest singer who has railed against everyone from Margaret Thatcher to Nicolas Sarkozy, credited with being the spokesman-elect of the *verlan*-speaking youth of the Paris suburbs before rap was invented.

page 29 BARDAMU Semi-autobiographical protagonist of *Voyage au bout de la nuit* by Louis-Ferdinand Céline (1894–1961).

page 49 MARCEL AYMÉ (1902–1967) French novelist, children's writer, humorist, playwright and screenplay writer. Aymé wrote about his native Franche-Comté as well as working-class Paris.

page 54 BAOUS A range of limestone hills in the Alpes-Maritimes department in south-east France.

page 55 ARSÈNE LUPIN Fictional gentleman-thief created by the writer Maurice Leblanc (1864–1941) in his long-running detective series. Leblanc was a contemporary of Conan Doyle, and Lupin – a force for good operating on the wrong side of the law – proved as popular in francophone countries as Sherlock Holmes in the English-speaking world.

page 59 FRANÇOIS TRUFFAUT (1932–1984) Leading film-maker and a founder of the French New Wave. The line about the dead mother, the ultimate excuse served up to a teacher, is taken from Truffaut's feature-film début *Les Quatre Cents Coups* (1959), a semi-autobiographical portrayal of a troubled Parisian adolescence.

page 59 MARIGNAN The Battle of Marignan (1515) was an episode in the Italian Wars, started by Charles VIII in 1494 in a bid to control the Duchy of Milan. It marked the young French king's first victory in the opening year of his reign, but came at a terrible price: sixteen thousand dead in a matter of days. This is an easy date which every French student knows.

page 68 HOLOFERNES In *Gargantua and Pantagruel* by François Rabelais (1494–1553), the giant Gargantua's tutor, Doctor Holofernes, represents a satire of rote-style medieval education.

page 68 PONCRATES By contrast, in the tutor Poncrates, Rabelais satirizes the shift to "enlightened" and analytical Renaissance scholasticism.

page 75 SPIROU The main character of the Belgian *Spirou et Fantasio* and *Le Petit Spirou* comic strips, created by Robert Velter ("Rob-Vel", 1909–1991) for the launch of the magazine *Le Journal de Spirou* in 1938. Unlike his compatriot Tintin, Spirou the journalist is often seen reporting back for his magazine as he finds himself caught up in yet another adventure.

page 75 SIGNES DE PISTE Children's pocket-book series, originally created in 1937 by the leader of the French scout movement and principally comprising novels featuring scouts.

page 75 BOB MORANE Adventure series created in 1953 by the Belgian novelist Henri Vernes (one of the pseudonyms used by Charles-Henri-Jean Dewisme, born 1918), who penned over two hundred novels featuring the eponymous hero. These led to a television series, an animated series and a long-running series of graphic novels.

page 83 JULES SUPERVIELLE (1884–1960) Uruguayan-born French poet, dramatist and short-story writer.

page 84 RICARDO GÜIRALDES (1886–1927) Argentine novelist and poet. *Don Segundo Sombra*, written in 1926, is set among the gauchos.

page 107 BLANC-MESNIL A suburban town north-east of Paris.

page 136 RAMEAU'S NEPHEW, *or the Second Satire* is an imaginary philosophical conversation written by Denis Diderot (1713–1784), probably between 1761 and 1772.

page 150 MEURSAULT The Outsider of Albert Camus' existential novel *L'Etranger* (1942), who seemingly without motive kills an Arab and faces execution.

page 171 PIERRE DE MARIVAUX (1688–1763) One of France's most important eighteenth-century comic playwrights. The term *Marivaudage* has been coined to describe the dramatist's lashing together of ornate and vernacular language, so that characters whom an audience might expect to speak in a high register suddenly make utterances in a low one. This playful relationship between social status and language makes Marivaux's play *Le Jeu de l'hasard et de l'amour* an apt choice for the teacher who stages it with her *banlieue* students in Abdellatif Kechiche's film *L'Esquive.*

page 171 L'ESQUIVE Or *Games of Love and Chance* (2003), film directed by the French-Tunisian filmmaker Abdellatif Kechiche.

page 177 FRANÇOIS VILLON (1431–disappeared 1463) Poet, thief, and vagabond. Largely unknown in his time and rediscovered in the sixteenth century, his best-known works are *Testament* and *La Ballade des pendus* (The Ballad of the Hanged Men), written while in prison.

page 184 MALAUSSÈNE Daniel Pennac's *Malaussène Saga* (sometimes dubbed the Belleville Quartet, although it comprises five novels and two shorter works) centres on the misadventures of Benjamin Malaussène, a professional scapegoat, hired by businesses to take their flak. There are also supporting turns from drug addicts, tattoo artists and the owner of the last theatre in Belleville in a portrayal that celebrates the diversity of this quarter of Paris. *La Fée carabine*, the second book in the series (1987), was translated as *The Fairy Gunmother* (1997).

page 208 LA PRINCESSE DE CLÈVES (1678) Seen by many as the first French novel and a prototype of the early psychological novel, it was published anonymously, though its author is widely thought to have been Madame de la Fayette (1634–1693). Since Pennac published *Chagrin d'école*, La Fayette's protracted tale of thwarted love has become a symbol of resistance to Sarkozy's restructuring of the French education system. The president having declared the civil-service entrance exams so antiquated that they even contained a question on *La Princesse de Clèves*, in 2009 university lecturers held public readings of the novel across France.

page 208 ALPHONSE DAUDET (1840–1897) Novelist, short-story writer, playwright, poet and literary syphilitic whose prose has often been likened to that of Charles Dickens. His autobiographical novel *Le Petit Chose* (1868), translated into English as *Little Good-For-Nothing* (1885) and *Little What's-His-Name* (1898), takes its title from the nickname given its narrator at school.

page 234 LE JEU DES MILLE EUROS France's longest-running radio quiz game, created in 1958. Listeners provide the questions, which are categorized as red, white or blue according to difficulty.

page 236 JEAN PIAGET (1896–1980) Swiss educationalist and director of the International Bureau of Education in Geneva from 1929 until 1967. His theory of cognitive development defined distinct developmental stages for children and led to a more "child-centred" approach to education in both Europe and America in the 1970s and '80s.

page 245 OGINO METHOD Calendar-based method of gauging a woman's fertility, whether to achieve or avoid pregnancy.

page 246 MICHEL AUDIARD (1920–1985) French screenwriter and film director, whose dialogue captured popular Parisian cheek and wit, particularly the irreverence of the 1960s.

Permissions

Extract from “La Sagesse du cancre” (“The Wisdom of the Dunce”), a short story by Marcel Aymé, taken from *Oeuvre romanesque complètes* volume 1 (Éditions Gallimard, Bibliothèque de la Pléiade, 2007), translated by Sarah Ardizzone.

Extract from *Le Livre de ma mere* by Albert Cohen, in an English translation by Bella Cohen entitled *Book of My Mother* (1999). Reproduced by permission of Peter Owen Ltd, London.

Extract from *Les Charactères* by Jean de la Bruyère, Chapter 9, “Des Grands”, in an English translation and with an introduction by Jean Stewart, *Characters* (Penguin Classics, 1970), Copyright © Jean Stewart, 1970. Reproduced by permission of Penguin Books, London.

“L’Allée”, a poem by Jules Supervielle, translated by Moniza Alvi as “In the Lane” in her *After Jules Supervielle* series. Reproduced by permission of Moniza Alvi.

Extract from *Adolphe* by Benjamin Constant, in a translation by Carl Wildman, with an introduction by Harold Nicolson (Hamish Hamilton, 1948). Copyright © Carl Wildman.

Extract from *Émile* by Jean-Jacques Rousseau, in a translation by William H. Payne, 1892 (Prometheus Books, 2003). Reproduced by permission of Prometheus Books, New York.

"L'Enfant et le maître d'école" ("The Child and the Schoolmaster") by Jean de La Fontaine, *Fables*, Book 1, XIX. Copyright © Guido Waldman, 2010. Reproduced by permission of Guido Waldman.

Extract from *Le Petit Chose* by Alphonse la Daudet, translated as *Little What's-His-Name* by Jane Minot Sedgewick (Little, Brown and Company, 1898).

Translator's Acknowledgements

This translation is for my husband, Simon – Daniel and Minne know how much.

And with boundless gratitude to Daniel.

Profonds remerciements go to Géraldine D'Amico, fairy godmother *par excellence*, for introducing me to the astonishing world of Monsieur Pennac and for brainstorming *Chagrin d'école* with infinite patience and laughter; to Jonathon Green, king of slang and a terrific Pennac advocate; to George May, for his enlightening Bath University M.A. on *Chagrin d'école* (and whose translation illuminated chapters 7 and 8 of Part 2); to the one and only Caz Royds of Walker Books, who taught me so passionately how to edit a Pennac translation, and to my editor, Andrea Belloli, a wonderful new encounter; to the fine team at MacLehose Press: Christopher MacLehose, Katharina Bielenberg and Nicci Praça; also to Christine Baker at Gallimard Jeunesse for her unstinting and treasured support; and of course to Quentin Blake, for another exquisite cover and Pennac collaboration.

And, finally, for the two teachers who turned my world right side up: Paul Hoffman and Lizzie Marsden.